AF615927

*The Imagination of Reference*

UNIVERSITY OF FLORIDA HUMANITIES MONOGRAPH 66

# *The Imagination of Reference*

## Meditating the Linguistic Condition

EDOUARD MOROT-SIR

*University Press of Florida*

GAINESVILLE • TALLAHASSEE • TAMPA • BOCA RATON
PENSACOLA • ORLANDO • MIAMI • JACKSONVILLE

Printed in the United States of America on acid-free paper ∞



Library of Congress Cataloging-in-Publication Data

Morot-Sir, Edouard.
The imagination of reference: meditating the linguistic condition/Edouard Morot-Sir.
p. cm. —(University of Florida humanities monograph; 16)
Includes bibliographical references and index.
ISBN 0–8130–1171–X
1. Reference (Philosophy) 2. Language and languages—Philosophy. 3. Philosophy, Modern. I. Title. II. Series: University of Florida monographs. Humanities; no. 66.
B105.R25M67 1993
149′.94—dc20 92–22881

The University Press of Florida is the scholarly publishing agency for the State University System of Florida, comprised of Florida A & M University, Florida Atlantic University, Florida International University, Florida State University, University of Central Florida, University of Florida, University of North Florida, University of South Florida, and University of West Florida.

University Press of Florida
15 Northwest 15th Street
Gainesville, FL 32611

*To Jacqueline*

*and Catherine*

# *Contents*

# Preface

The first idea of this research goes back to the early fifties when I was assessing the epistemological limits of my *Pensée négative* and becoming conscious of the deadlock where modern idealisms, from Kant to Léon Brunschvicg and Gaston Bachelard, from David Hume to Edmund Husserl, were stamping. Then, my project was delayed by turns in my academic career, first my involvement in Paris and in New York in Franco-American cultural affairs and later, my teaching in French literature and criticism. A welcome delay and detour—seminars in Tucson and Chapel Hill, particularly on Pascal, surrealism, Proust, and Samuel Beckett—helped me to elaborate new methodological perspectives on my continuous and subjacent reflection on language. May I express my gratitude to my students whose critical enthusiasm maintained my faith in my work and helped to overcome periods of doubt and discouragement.

In the late seventies I had the strange urge to swim against the main philosophical current. In the Anglo-Saxon world fashion leaned no more toward the theory of language but toward the philosophy of mind. In literary criticism other fashions were invading teaching in the humanities under the labels of structuralism and deconstructionism. A new wave of French philosophers, influenced more or less by Marx, Nietzsche, Freud, Heidegger, and Bataille, was playing brilliant variations on the death of Man and his language. The paradoxes of their critical radicalism helped me to pursue my own way of meditation and to regain confidence in the few certitudes I was entertaining, even if I had the ambiguous feeling of the woodsman opening a few clearings in the forest of language.

I owe a debt of deep gratitude to Raymond Gay-Crosier, chairman of the Humanities Series at UPF. He was the first to read my manuscript; his generous belief in my work brought me very precious encouragements, and I am also grateful for his valuable comments and suggestions. I would also like to express my warmest thanks to the editors of University Press of Florida for the thorough, precise, and comprehensive work they have done on my manuscript.

De quoi s'agissait-il donc? De rien moins que de retrouver le secret d'un langage dont les éléments cessassent de se comporter en épaves à la surface d'une mer morte . . . On n'a jamais assez insisté sur le sens de l'opération qui tendait à restituer le langage à sa vraie vie, soit bien mieux que de remonter de la chose signifiée au signe qui lui survit, ce qui s'avèrerait impossible, de se reporter d'un bond à la naissance du signifiant.

André Breton,
*Manifeste du surréalisme*

What was it all about then? Nothing less than the rediscovery of the secret of a language whose elements would then cease to float like jetsam on the surface of a dead sea. . . . Not enough attention has been paid to the meaning and the scope of the operation which tended to bring language back to life: in other words, rather than go back from the thing signified to the sign that lives after it (which, moreover, would prove to be impossible) it is better to go back in one leap to the birth of that which signifies. (Translated by R. Seaver and Helen R. Lane.)

D'Arthez avait une oeuvre d'imagination, entreprise uniquement pour étudier les ressources de la langue. Ce livre, encore inachevé, pris et repris par caprice, il le gardait pour les jours de grande détresse. C'était une oeuvre psychologique et de haute portée sous la forme du roman.

Honoré de Balzac,
*Les Illusions perdues*

D'Arthez had a work of imagination uniquely undertaken to study the properties of language. This book, yet unfinished, capriciously taken back again and again, he reserved for the days of great distress. It was a psychological work of great range under the form of a novel.

En d'autres termes, c'est le langage qui aurait créé l'homme, plutôt que l'homme le langage. . . .

Jacques Monod,
*Le Hasard et la nécessité*

In other terms, it is language that created man, rather than man language. . . .

Fiction is the vital element of phenomenology. . . .

Edmund Husserl

# MEDITATION ONE

## *Walking Through the Linguistic Narthex*

### *Writing, Self-Examination, and Meditation*

My introductory metaphor of a linguistic narthex* aims at the image of language as the cathedral of words, a world by itself, surrounding human individuals (my writing, the present words included), a world that is more than a corpus of images, ideas, and rules with instrumental power, a true cosmos with impassable borders for the one who would claim to enter it or get out of it. It depends on me, on you, to be its faithful, reluctant, or skeptical servant, attendant, choirboy, or priest. At times of great exaltation I, you, can feel that we have become the architect-master of its infinite composition and harmony, with invisible walls, a world that I, you, apprehend at each moment of our active and dreaming lives as a strict system of already prepared programs or as an open temptation. Whatever our forceful choices or humble submissions may be, for us there is always a continuous insight of initiation, a sense of permanent rediscovery and surprise. It is as if we were at first catechumens waiting for some passport permitting us to be accepted in the true continent of knowledge and reality.

Before going further, may I state once and for all that my search for analogies and my insistence on them is deliberate; the process I am practicing and plan to pursue throughout the present endeavor, process of magnifying similes and metaphors, has the value of a methodological caveat: since it is impossible to think, that is to say, to put words in relational systems, without implying analogical connections, it seems intellectually more honest to plead guilty and to force metaphors to expose themselves in the forefront and to cry out their identities.

*Any reference to linguistic expressions in themselves, without implications of an independent referent and meaning, will be marked by single apostrophes. Double apostrophes will serve as usual to indicate quotations, such as expressions borrowed from real or imaginary languages.

Our metaphoric game belongs to the consciousness of a preliminary situation for anyone who aspires to recapture language in its spirit and universality. Obvious, but most often ignored, this state of affairs is not an object I can scrutinize as I would a small-print piece of writing through a magnifying glass. *Its* examination is *my* examination; *its* exposition is *my* confession. Even the most radical linguist with semiotic safety blinders cannot escape this general precondition: simultaneously language is my language, yours, theirs. Phenomenologists call this condition "intersubjectivity." Indeed, it is intersubjectivity with the omnipresence of the three personal pronouns, singular and plural, but, *within* my, your, their subjectivity; even at certain moments, each of us believes that he/she has reached a pure expression of objectivity. Let us draw this simple consequence: there can be no study of language without a *preliminary self-examination*.

The selection of a title, in spite of its being publicity-oriented, is a very subjective matter and often the expression of hidden expectations. For my own project, many titles were tried. I began with the intent of writing about "writing philosophy." During the last ten years I organized my own imaginary laboratory mostly with a few French philosophers or writers, as exemplary cases for crucial testing—Pascal, Sartre, Merleau-Ponty, Bataille, Malraux, and Camus. One day, at the same time as a few others were interested in the relation between linguistics and philosophy, I found out that the problem of meaning, as important as it was, should be subordinated to the problem of reference, understood as the *double linguistic experience of truth and reality*. Dealing with my illustrious guinea pigs, I realized also that, whatever the topic of their writing may have been, they always tried to answer, indirectly or not, the question, "What is language?" Behind an anthology, a philosophy of perception, a world vision, and so on, a practical philosophy of language appeared in filigree and actually gave its last word to radical efforts of renewing philosophy. Writing philosophy ultimately means ascribing to modern languages new semantic and lexical powers, in order to grasp a new meaningful and referencing existence. Merleau-Ponty speaks of the "slippery grasp that literature gives to us on experience".[1] It could be added that the main function of philosophical language is to try to change a slippery grasp into a firm, secure possession.

Little by little I was led to a conclusion that served as a true springboard for further investigations: from Pascal to Malraux, from Descartes to Sartre, passing through Hume, Kant, and romanticism, modern European philosophers and essayists have been obsessed by the "imaginary" of human civilizations. Imagination has been seen by all of them as the villain or the hero of the Human Comedy. Living and practical paradoxes, my experimental models were facing an ultimate question, "How can one reconcile the double exigency of a philosophical language in itself and its literary suckers—the building up of abstract or concrete imaginaries and the awareness of being in tune with Being—and thus how can one balance in the same act the pleasure of the imaginary and the ascetic imperative of reference?" One day I understood that between imagination and reference there was no actual conflict. On the contrary, they were respective accessories in the making of human history. That explains the title chosen as label for these pages, "The Imagination of Reference," where "of" brings more suggestive power than the usual "and" so much appreciated by philosophers. I merrily accept the ambiguity of that "of" whose only purpose is to rouse an infinite field of relations between imagination and reference. Let us start the game: the act of imagining reference, the imaginary quality of reference, the act of referring to imagination, reference as the imagination of the referents, imagination as the consciousness of reference, the coincidence between the imaginary world and the indexical system of references, and so on. I just hope that my present exercise will help in shaping a few roads in that semantic complexity. Completing this presentation of my title, I add that I am more than aware that, when I begin to write "the imagination of reference," I am subjecting myself to a convergent intellectual redoubling: at the same time, to imagine what I dare to call the imagination of reference, and to index its products, as if imagining and indexing were one and the same.

My confidence is more apparent than real! I am not invoking a sudden illumination, one of those famous inspired "intuitions" that set fire to the forest of language and lay out new clearings. More modestly I feel that I have reached a point of culmination, as if my effort to make my consciousness language-obsessed and to change any linguistic experience into an immense interrogation mark, was weakening and ready to be converted into more or less declarative writing. I apologize for being so self-centered and insisting so much, at the outset, on my very subjective readiness, which after all should be of no concern to the occasional reader. . . . Only to a point, and that is my excuse: I deeply believe that the act of writing on language at a nonscientific level cannot help being both declarative and performative, serene contemplation and painstaking intelligence and self-realization, both solliciting others' similar actions. Scientists write notes about already completed experiments. The philosopher makes of his note an experiment lived by himself or herself and, he or she hopes, one to be lived by others. In brief, writing philosophy is not describing, explaining events after they happened, and validating a few predictions.

No responsible car owner drives without a driver's license delivered by proper authorities. Indeed, writing permits, in the form of academic titles, do exist: "I am a Ph.D. and that gives me the right to publish even at high speed." However, as is well known, such permits are not absolutely required. Critics as policemen of letters, intervene to say that a writer should or should not have made the decision to publish. At least, in our liberal societies, the decision to write remains an intersubjective and personal affair. It starts with a general need and the awareness of a proper and mature moment. . . . I am just trying to invoke my philosophical need and my feeling of a long-awaited and specific maturity. Another factor really played the role of trigger when doubts emerged about the urgency of the need for writing, or the right time for doing it: "I feel competent! And I hope that my own work will prove it." Usually this problem of competence is not discussed, except after the sin of writing has already been committed, and it is the responsibility of the critic to recognize or deny legitimate competence. It would be in very bad taste to warn one's reader and to state in a foreword: "May I reassure you of my competence for such and such reason!" Indeed a proper name by itself can be such a declaration or implication of competence. The decision not to give names, but only titles on the cover would indeed change the world of publishing! In any case, although aware of that dubious situation, I think that I cannot avoid such a preliminary declaration of limited competence, for a simple reason: today when a writer decides not to abide strictly by the laws of linguistics, and especially, when his or her writing becomes a deliberate effort not to be guided by those laws, theories of language lie at the crossroads of at least four distinctive and required competencies: history of philosophy, present theories of language, literary criticism, and, last but not least, linguistics. My experience as reader in this general field has shown me that, even in the best cases, works are usually based on a maximum of two competencies, or two and a half. The most frequently expected and satisfied ones are strong competencies in the theory of language and linguistics, with a limited information on the history of philosophy and an obvious ignorance of literary criticism. Let us consider two illustrious examples. Even if one disagrees with his theses, one will not question Chomsky's competence in linguistics; but one could express reservations about the validity of his interpretation of Cartesianism and of the Enlightenment, and one would deplore the absence of literary references in his works. With strong differences within those specialties, John Searle seems to follow the same pattern. For example, when he harshly condemns Derrida's deconstructionism, he aptly demonstrates his skill in philosophical debates; but he reveals his weakness in literary criticism. Because of a missing background, his active memory has not succeeded in integrating the cultural forces that have generated the success of Derrida in the seventies, however objectionable it may be.

Indeed a talented writer can brilliantly hide or surmount informational deficiencies. Furthermore, too much competency could turn useless erudition. In our modern cultural training, most thinkers have developed from a basic competency obtained during their student years. On the way they have tried to append a few other specialties to their cart. . . . As for me, with a basic training in epistemology and in the history of Western philosophies, I was constantly in touch with the successive literary revolutions of the twentieth century, and after 1950 I worked hard at compensating my early ignorance of linguistics. I am well aware that I shall always remain in the narthex of that science, even if, after many years of puzzling perplexities, I can understand how the mind of linguists ticks and how their methodological requirements give shape to their basic concepts. In other words, I mean to warn you that I will approach the problematic of language from the epistemological point of view, being strongly conscious of the philosophical and literary movements that contributed to forming our cultures and the ceaseless reincarnations of their languages. As for linguistics, I plan to borrow its vocabulary, to discuss the present state of its hypotheses, but I shall not claim to write on behalf of the ideal of scientific truth, with a behaviorist, physicalist, or mentalist model.

This point of departure bears a few remarkable consequences for the process of writing. First, it concerns the relation to the infinite of linguistic experiences, which should be the permanent preoccupation of the philosophy of language as well as of linguistics. The latter likes to invent well-formed, or not, sentences borrowed from the common language, on the famous type of *La plume de ma tante* or "snow is white," and to experiment on them. Such examples serve as illustrations. In no way are they comparable to the laboratory experiments of biology, which can validate or not hypotheses. They belong neither to the current usage of human communication nor to the literary forms of culture. I do not blindly reject that experimental technique. It is probably convenient for linguists; but it has no real value for the philosopher. Thus, when they will be called for, my examples will stay at a strictly empirical level; they will come from observation of daily life or from actual literary or philosophical texts. Depriving the philosopher of the facile reference to texts that seem to be only pale imitations of scientific discourse, I must face the consequence of that state of writing: philosophical writing must not expect to follow the patterns of demonstrative or narrative linearity. Even when he believes he is writing his autobiography, a philosopher never tells a story, or he ceases to be a philosopher. Hegel's *Phenomenology of Spirit* is the history of Western consciousness on the surface of the text only. Actually, it is a systematization and totalization of modern European languages, transcending time in a sort of critical imaginary. Does this mean that history has been converted by Hegel into a powerful demonstration? No, because the dialectical process imagined by Hegel as synthetic or linking power is an artificial genesis. Dialectics proves nothing. It is supposed to *show* the inevitability of a certain experience made by my consciousness in the effort to master its subjectivity. No philosophical discourse can succeed in taking the shape of deductive or inductive orders. Spinoza failed in his efforts to give the *Ethics* the appearance of Euclidian geometry. In contemporary philosophy too many pages are devoted to "prove" the errors committed by other philosophers. Nothing is really proved except the fact of a change in the intellectual mood: all those very complex argumentations go no further than a brilliant show of sophistic gifts.

However, well hidden in the middle of endless quibbles, lies authentic philosophy in its unashamed subjectivity. Then, there are no more denunciations of errors or affirmations of truth. There is only the evidence of an experience within language. Following in Montaigne's steps, Descartes gave an example that, since then, has rarely been repeated in its specific form, except by Husserl with his *Cartesian Meditations*. After his *Discourse on Method*—an autobiography under the guise of a temporary publication presenting samples of different kinds of research in metaphysics, mathematics, and the natural sciences—Descartes, with the six *Meditations,* proposed a model for all future philosophers to follow, the model of a philosophical language that does not pretend to compete with scientific languages. Even when he committed himself to "prove" the existence of the human mind, of God and Space, he rejected the syllogistic formulation, and imposed on philosophical discourse the obligation to say "I" as the universal subject of metaphysical language. In doing so, he implicitly recognized that his so-called "meditations" were actually and essentially meditations, subjective, direct, and lived experiences reorganizing the basic concepts of modern languages. Then, the process of meditation emerged, pure and unspoiled, from the combined structures—old and new—of logic, rhetoric, and dialectic. Negatively speaking, this is a sort of *deimplication* of living language, an unveiling of its codes and forms; it is a return to the sources or principles of Sense and Being. Husserl understood the originality of the meditative process better than any other philosopher before or after him. His analysis of the phenomenological method should be for us the point of departure for a new comprehension of *language as meditation*. However, the Husserlian "epochè," as intellectual askesis and purification, is limited to the two-level suspension of perception and of conceptual meaning. Today, half a century later, we have to go further and apply the radical power of suspension, neutralization, or *uncapping* to the basic words of our linguistic condition. That will be our first endeavor after leaving the narthex.

Husserl furthermore believed that the term "description" could qualify for philosophical investigations in opposition to the hypothetico-deductive order of sciences or the dialectical illusion of modern idealisms. But the decision to describe implies the belief in something to be described. That implication is inacceptable when one deals with basic words. Occasionally a basic word can be described empirically. Such a process belongs to the domains of intellectual psychology, sociology of culture, history of ideas, or anthropology. Indeed the reports of those human scientists are useful, especially in preparing oneself for meditation; but meditation itself is the prolonged apprehension of the original language per se, the progressive awareness of its *necessity* as cluster of self-imposed originary obligations. Meditation is thus the awareness of the basic words *before* philosophy attempts to regroup them into a system, but Pascal, meditating on Cartesian innate ideas, warned us:

> Ainsi quand ils [les principes] sont tous renfermés en un ils y sont cachés et inutiles, comme en un coffre et ne paraissent jamais qu'en leur confusion naturelle. La nature les a tous établis, sans renfermer l'un dans l'autre.
>
> [Thus when they (the principles) are all enclosed within one they are hidden there and useless, as in a chest, and they appear only in their natural confusion. Nature has established all of them, without confining one into the other.][2]

Capital warning, unheard by three centuries of furious and intense attempts at linguistic systematization by Western philosophers, with the few exceptions of Diderot, Kierkegaard, Husserl, Nietzsche, and his French version, Georges Bataille—but fortunately understood by mathematicians and mathematical physicists, who, each in his or her respective domain, worked on their basic words and the possibility—or impossibility—of their organization and administration.

My present problem is not to try to show the importance of these great protesters. It has already been done by those who call themselves "deconstructionists." But, in spite of their intellectual usefulness, they do not go back to the radicalism of the first steps realized by Descartes; they are systematic antisystematizers; they never remain at this primitive level of sense-and-reference, they discuss only others' flaws.

Meditative life subsists in our daily existence of physical actions and communications, although it remains in the background, hidden behind our opened exterior or interior discourse, or intervening very briefly, in exceptional moments, like an evanescent particle of our mental energy. Thus my present duty will be to make meditation present in a special language that I call philosophy.

Consequently when I *speak* of meditation, I refer to a typical philosophical *language,* a linguistic writing process, not a psychological behavior. The possibility of a psychological theory of meditation, if not excluded, is reserved, suspended. The meditations to come will be a totality of linguistic developments conducted in English, which is not my native language, needless to say. I discarded the easy solution of a meditation in French to be translated by an English or American scholar because, even though the probability of grammatical mistakes and Gallic turns of phrase will always be very high, I have to experience the principles of language with my English vocabulary and grammar instead of relying on a translator. Direct practice of English has another advantage: although more than fifty percent of my primary sources, such as linguistic laboratory experiments, will be French, the proportion is reversed for secondary sources. As is well known, this is due to the enormous amount of research on the problem of language in English-speaking countries. Thus, just trying to be fair to all those language philosophers and to limit their Frenchization, my reflections should be given in English: I should not have the choice of weapons. I also found an advantage in conducting meditations in English instead of French, even if I have and will continue to have many lapses and relapses: in my experience writing in French I must confess that I am unable to separate phonetics from lexicon or syntax, and none of them from semantic and rhetorical habits; I float in a sort of translucent matter, insidiously too absorbing. On the contrary, I had no problem indeed in feeling and trying very distinctly the challenge and resistance of English phonetics, vocabulary, and grammar. May I confess that Roget's *Thesaurus of Words and Phrases* does not leave my desk! Let us hope that, after so many pages in English I will be able to push to its expressive limit my present meditation, and the experience of the imagination of reference.

## *Methodological Quandaries and Intricacies*

1. The choice of a philosophical language has just been made, and this language is called 'meditation.' I am ready to admit that it is hardly a methodological decision compared with the usual scientific rules. We clearly know what meditation is not: it rejects the general, linear, hypothetico-deductive pattern; it looks for experiences that are foreign to perceptual observations and physical experiments; it changes the current, fluid transparency of signifiers into semiotic opacity, linguistic instrumentality into organized reverie of thought; it strives to overcome the practical duality of thinking and acting. Little by little the "meditator" becomes conscious of his meditation as close to the reverie of poets and mystics, as a secret omnipresent force, if rarely recognized, as language speaking to and for itself. It reminds me of the dream of surrealism of finding a point beyond the great antinomies of human condition, beyond language itself. It is a sort of paradoxical "automatic writing," because, as André Breton superbly wrote, it intends "to go back in one leap to the birth of that which signifies." Meditation hopes to recover spaces and times in intense, ineffable moments of silence, so that its writings aspire to the humble status of a shadow accompanying and arousing the brilliant lights of what theological language calls "eternal beatitude." Thus, more than any other linguistic conduct, meditation is reduplicating itself in a back-and-forth movement between writing-meditation and living-meditation. The temptation of furtively passing from one to the other is almost inevitable, and it is the source of many literary or philosophical complacencies. Here rises up a serious caveat that should remain present in the development of my meditative writing. *Never trespass meditation!* In spite of an imperious desire to transcend language, meditating must strictly stay as a pure writing performance and endeavor, especially when it writes about silence or any other existential emptiness. In homage to Descartes, let us name this universal caveat *the imperative of linguistic evidence*.

2. There is another temptation that threatens meditative life and writing. It is the *seduction of virtuality.* Reference to virtuality is the most frequent trap in our intellectual life on a seesaw between past and future virtualities, a constant reference to potentialities trying to explain the passage from one point to another, from one moment to another. Blessed virtuality intervenes to unlock the wheels of the linguistic operation when they risk being immobilized by the Parmenidian dichotomy of Being and Nothingness: between them, surrounding them, the ocean of virtualities carries floats made of words. There is no poetic language without an invitation to symbolic virtualities. One may also remember that, after Descartes' elimination of the concepts of force and energy, they were restored one generation later by Leibniz, who changed qualitative virtualities into mathematical symbols. Such a conversion was responsible for the success of classical mechanics and the development of the physical sciences; but, again and again, philosophers, not impressed by the triumphal progress of modern technology, contested the Leibnizian change: virtualities as qualities, philosophers insist, are not convertible into well-defined concepts and words referring to beings.

When, after discarding the problem of the origin of language as nonscientific, linguistics tried to go beyond cautious historico-descriptive methodology, and to surpass its status of empirical knowledge, when it decided to face again the problem of the original inventiveness of language, it was inevitable that it make an effort to invoke linguistic virtuality and, for that purpose, that it rely on the high-security jail of the notion of structure. Maybe Noam Chomsky is more Leibnizian than Cartesian! His distinctions between deep and surface structures, between linguistic competence and performance are closer to Leibnizian dynamics than to Descartes' pure geometrism. "Competence" is another name for linguistic aptitude. Transformational and generative grammar determines the state and condition of language before expressed language. Thus, one understands Chomsky's strong opposition to a pure linguistic behaviorism à la Skinner, that is, a theory of language without reference to virtual capacities. But is it not a return to medieval occult forces, through an unavowed Leibnizianism? Cartesians of strict obedience reproached Leibniz his Aristotelian and Scholastic leniency.

To my comment, it could be objected that Chomsky's "mentalism" implies a physical basis, and thus, his famous distinctions are compatible with a linguistic brain-model. However, and without taking a stand for or against rational or empirical methodologies in their present state of generative grammar and theory of learning, the philosophy of language cannot avoid the problem of virtual existence as applied to language in its universal meaning and its multiple applications. The dilemma is clear, although not easy to solve. I cannot write without appealing to virtual qualities, but how can I experience them through meditation? To be more specific, there is no possible theory of reference without an understanding of linguistic virtualities, because any reference implies actual or virtual referents. But how can I refer to virtualities supporting and explaining a certain performance? For example, what is literary criticism if not the claim of unveiling the virtualities of a text? Depending on the theory favored, those virtualities will be called forms, deep structures, intentionalities, values, one way or another referring to a sort of Hidden God. Thus this new caveat: *keep your eyes open when dealing with lexical, grammatical, and semantic virtualities.* I say caveat, not interdiction, because I cannot avoid references to virtualities, provided I do not confuse them with simple virtual realities.

Related to that basic problem, is another nagging one when virtuality is referred to the presence of *semantic implications* in a given language. First, this is a fact of language: how can I speak or write without shadows of implications? Pascal is only partly right when he underlines the pluralism of the primitive words of knowledge, the impossibility of their reunification under a philosophical system, and their intellectual efficiency only when they are treated independently of one another. Then, he decides to ignore their constant overlap and communication. Sense is like a subterranean blood that feeds the life of concepts. There is a complex game of synonyms and antonyms, so that no word, even a proper name, can exist in proud isolation. Confusion is the inevitable consequence of interconceptual infusion and diffusion. Thus, the Cartesian requirement of clear and distinct ideas appears to be an ideal rarely reached except in the very abstract conditions of formal thinking or in the successful computerization of artificial intelligence. Human beings have learned to live and think within a more or less acute state of confusion. Pascal's effort of conceptual diffusion should be accompanied by a vivid awareness of the implications hidden behind the simplest sentence.

As a crucial example, let us consider the first two sentences of Wittgenstein's *Philosophical Grammar:* "How can one talk about 'understanding' and 'not understanding' a proposition? Surely it's not a proposition until it's understood?" Except for the word 'proposition' that belongs to the lexicon of logic and has a relatively clear definition (if clarity means its unequivocal usage), any other word used by Wittgenstein appertains to our daily vocabulary and offers multiple interpretations. "How" and "Surely" would plunge a disciple of Hume into an abyss of perplexities! What is the meaning of "being understood"? The experts know the Wittgensteinian answer. Is it possible to accept it without agreeing with many other philosophical suppositions? Now, to what experience does one refer when one speaks of "talking about"? Is "to talk" put for or instead of "to think" or "to reflect"? Does "talking" imply or not the possibility of "thinking"? And if so, what is the favored philosophical option? I know that one could always say that these questions are philosophical subtleties and that they never stopped the man of the street from "talking about" things and intentions. Is it not confessing the impossibility of an absolute control on semantic implications, and then, on the virtualities that accompany any kind of discourse? To continue with Wittgenstein's quotation, should we modify slightly his phrasing and say: "Surely it is not a true or false proposition until it is understood"? "True or false" can be judged redundant, because of the implied definition of "proposition." Again one feels the presence of a potential philosophical option, not to mention the verb "can" implying that language has a mysterious power, designated by the term "understanding." Indeed, there is an overlap between "producing linguistic signs" and "understanding them."

I could go on indefinitely, enumerating the implications of two simple well formed sentences both with question marks, but different grammatical form. Does it mean that any sensible person should advocate silence, communication with a few gestures, and ignore the deceptive versatilities of language? Such behaviors were seriously considered by the Cynic philosophers or, in a different mood, by the followers of Abbot de Rancé. However, this linguistic radicalism does not succeed in excluding the very fact of linguistic implication. As is well known, 'silence' signifies and possesses a strange referential power. Samuel Beckett had to write 260 pages to express the unnamability of his writing. . . . We can complete our caveat concerning the seduction of virtuality: by purifying our languages in pinpointing and denouncing dubious implications, one is threatened by two opposite consequences: to replace known implications by unknown ones in the simple fact of talking, or to cultivate a rhetoric of silence. There is only one certitude: *the recurrent dream of absolute beginning, of semantic virginity and immaculate conception is irrealizable*. Putting that dream in the form of a problem is not even advisable.

3. About thirty years ago, the French structuralism wave swept away the then well-established positivist and idealist epistemologies inherited

from Kant and Comte. It also proposed restoring the old or rejunevated vocabulary of rhetoric using Aristotle's textbooks as Bible. It was a refreshing change. Roman Jakobson's famous interpretation of the paradigmatic and syntagmatic structures of language in relation with the rhetorical duality of metaphor and metonymy stirred up the imagination of many a literary critic: it became belief that literary creation should be decomposed and restructured into rhetorical units. Dumarsais-Fontanier's textbook re-edited by Gérard Genette was added to Aristotle's *Rhetoric* and *Poetics*. . . . Today, one may wonder if the remedy was not worse than the disease it was supposed to cure. After three centuries of scornful rejection, the intervening of Rhetoric's vocabulary was done too hastily and without methodological reflection. Rhetorical terms were taken as primitive concepts when they were haphazard products of traditional description of literary forms. They had a problematic quality that was taken for heuristic power. One sympathizes with the laudable effort of the *Group Mu* that undertook to build up a new rhetoric on a systematic and formal basis; but philosophers and critics did not follow. Furthermore, the relation between rhetoric and epistemology was never clarified. There was an obvious need not only for a new rhetoric, but first, for a new philosophy of rhetoric. The epistemological and ontological implications of the vocabulary of rhetoric were not mastered, and the revival of the old lexicon created the illusion of new theoretical explanations.

I do not suggest that we should return to the beginning of the seventeenth century when any form of scholastic pedantry was condemned by Cartesians and Jansenists, and all rhetoric devices were reduced to metaphor. The awareness of the rhetorical work resulting from centuries of reflection on language and its literary applications is essential to the philosophy of language, except for one reservation: Rhetoric stays at the level of the most superficial description of language; at its best it is similar to the old botanical or zoological taxinomies. It is an homage to human ingenuity. It helps to change language from fact to problem. Thus, the following caveat: rhetoric contributes to remind the philosopher of a fact he or she has a tendency to forget: science is not the only goal of language, and *a treatise of rhetoric should not be confused with epistemology, or even with aesthetics*. It offers a very rich material to experiment with, nothing less and nothing more. Observing great writers shows that Pascal's famous saying about philosophy applies even better to rhetoric: true rhetoric laughs at rhetoric. Rhetoric should be grasped in its evolution, whereas treatises entertain the illusion of fixed and permanent forms. The status of the literary image in seventeenth-century texts is very different from the status it acquired at the beginning of the twentieth century through the successive innovations of romanticism and symbolism. Then, Dumarsais and Fontanier are of little help. Meditating on the powers of poetic language, Baudelaire, Rimbaud, and Mallarmé did not put forward theories. As critics or artists, they transcribed their personal sensibility of a given language and its powers. Mallarmé feels language to be "mobile et pourtant stable"[3] and he refers us to "l'instinct d'harmonie que, jeune ou grand, on a en soi" [mobile and yet stable . . . the instinct of harmony that, young or adult, one has within oneself].[4] In permanent contact with those direct, original experiences, philosophy of language can become a true experiment to the second degree.

4. Among the most important and elusive implications associated with the consciousness of language is the concept of *communication*. Obviously there is no human language or even any language at all without communication; but the reverse proposition is disputable and depends upon nominal definitions. André Martinet, in *Eléments de linguistique générale,* states as a postulate of linguistics that "la fonction principale de cet instrument qu'est une langue est celle de communication" [the essential function of that instrument that is a tongue is that of communication].[5] When Antoine Meillet in *Introduction à l'étude comparée des langues indo-européennes* defines language as a social system of associations and refuses to see in it the result of individual creations, he clearly implies the concept of communication. What does that general consensus among linguists mean? How can one understand this reciprocal causality: language is the instrument of communication, and in reverse, communication is the consequence of language? One could also speak in terms of finality and say that communication is the essential end of language. With such statements, the difficulty is not solved; it is only transferred to the neighboring concepts of "instrument" and "end"; I shall discuss later those notions. For the moment, I just issue a warning concerning the current assimilation of language and communication. A linguist can be satisfied with the vague observation that those two concepts are assimilable and proceed from initial confusion to precise intellectual conventions; but the philosopher of language's main reflection willy-nilly remain at the level of complex implications. His only sensible beginning should consist in ignoring the language-communication connection, as scandalous and difficult as it can be.

Let us consider a pragmatic definition of communication: "*Communication occurs when events in one place or at one time are closely related to events in another place or at another time.*"[26] It is the least biased definition of communication that one can imagine. It does not concern the essence of communication. It applies to its verifiable occurrences and requires only the concept of event with spatial or temporal dimensions, that is, the possibility of coexistence and succession. Apparently it is a good physical "description" except for the verbal phrase "are closely related." "Closely" cannot refer to the causal contact that was a problem for the seventeenth-century mechanism; "related" does not designate the relation of cause and effect. Are this adverb and this past participle means of speaking about language without implying other concepts than communication and thus a way to derive the concepts of designation, signification, and expression from a minimal relation? Pascal warned us that, as pleasant as it may be in its simplicity, and however useful it is for the elaboration of a physics of communication, such an intellectual coup de force cultivates a dangerous theoretical illusion, even for the understanding of communication itself. Then a new caveat can be specified: *beware of the too-easy assimilation of language and communication,* especially when evaluating the scientific theory of communication and information. Watch out for the slightest irreducible difference. At least, for a while, and as long as the present meditation has not exposed the varied primitive words that regulate our relations with language and human cultures, let us never forget that language and communication are distinct processes, even if it is impossible to find one without the other, one playing the role of an instrument for the other. Let us try to make language aware of itself independently of our need for communication.

5. I have refrained and suspended the usual practices of linear order for any kind of language processing, be it deductive, inductive, or dialectical. Doing so, I admit that meditation must contain and fight the temptation of system organization as expression and completion of its personal writing. Systematization or theory building is contrary to the spirit of philosophical reflection. Only sciences, thanks to their own methodological requirements, can dream of an absolute system of knowledge, even if it must be projected into a very distant future. Such a dream can be partially satisfied with theories limited and regional in their ambition, in spite of their imperialistic and reductionist tendencies. That was the Cartesian lesson, mostly misunderstood because Descartes himself and his successors for two centuries were fascinated by the Encyclopedic gathering of all sciences. If that aspiration had been limited to the sciences and their applications, the damage would not have been serious. Unfortunately philosophy was involved in this modern venture.

Is meditation as nonsystemized thinking possible? Is a philosophy of language possible without developing itself into a regional or universal theory? It is relatively easy to contain the movement toward the unification of thought and to decide to express oneself along a fragmentary line, but it is less easy to fight against the belief in a secret descending line toward the safety and firmness of solid foundations. That sort of architectural metaphor is rarely absent from the thinker's imagination, be he or she philosopher or scientist. It is a sort of practical linguistic rule, the best decision a language can make for sparing itself from falling into pure dissemination of knowledge. It is the Cartesian dream of a solid rock on which I could anchor myself and my discourse or upon which I could rely to build up the Palace of Sciences or to root the Tree of Knowledge. Images swarm up to suggest the same and universal need for a primal place from which to start or to return discourses. It is not the first point at the beginning and origin of an horizontal line; it is the deepest point of a vertical ascension or descent.

At this "point" I urge a *Foundation-suspension,* with the following advice: *to develop language without horizontal or vertical beginnings, and also without the seductive shelter of logical or hermeneutical circularity.*

6. It should be noted that, hoping to extricate myself from all sorts of insidious presuppositions, I return again and again to the word 'language,' in the same manner as theologians return to the word 'being.' I confess that I refer constantly to language as if I knew what it meant, when actually I have in my mind little more than the occurrence of this very word 'language.' Is there a kind of practical definition? Discarding all those properties that help philosophers and linguists to qualify language, may I say that, for the moment, language is just the term I have to use when I cannot think with specificity and precision! It is as if 'language' was just the secret, ultimate and unknown subject and object of my sentences. Any finished discourse would appear in the following form, "Language is such that (. . .) *y* (*fx*) in any language." Thus, I call for a methodological decision of *linguistic agnosticism;* not the skepticism of the Greek tradition; not the relativism of modern obedience; not the submission in front of a Kantian unknowable designating "language in itself" instead of the famous "thing in itself"; but simply the awareness that language, being the unique source of all the knowledge stored in our civilizations, can be neither their incarnations nor their final cultural depository, as it is often said. I speak of the English or the French languages, their respective qualities, their tendencies, and their limits in vocabulary and grammar. Each time I observe

something about them, the word 'language' appears as unknown subject or object, specifying sentences but itself remaining unspecified. I can live with and accept that state of affairs, as long as I confess it and do not smuggle semantic goods.

I will not forget my initial remark about the status of 'language' similar to that of 'being' in theological texts and in historical languages when they are more than signal-exchanges. Why not, then, obey common sense and speak of language as of being? The preceding formula could be written this way: "the being of language is such that . . . in any linguistic being and part of being." Grammar, logic, sciences of all kinds imply that formula and live very well with it. But, if it is permitted to take that step, a philosophy of language would destroy itself and turn its initial critical and radical intent into regional science or journalistic mediocrity. Indeed, it is too early to discuss the relation of 'language' to 'being' or the meaning of the phrase 'linguistic being.' I cannot claim to avoid such existential questions. I only hope to avoid the historical bias that made the success of Western thought and its impressive performances. Such is the present caveat: *let us never deal with language as being or quality of being transportable into grammatical subject and object,* but let us call upon the word 'language' each time we need to protect ourselves against any ontological or axiological presuppositions. For example, saying "God is *causa sui,*" I should immediately add that it is just a manner of speaking; I should make the same correction when I say: "I see a somptuous cardinal pecking seeds at my birdfeeder": these are just words. The occurrence of the word 'language' or its synonyms, thus uncapped again and again, will become for me the recurrent signal of a *methodological nominalism* that is the expression of the linguistic agnosticism I just recommend to myself. As a consequence, *references to language will be ways to declare and live my ignorance;* the phrase "to be only language" will be a constant warning that the universal ontological trespassing that posits the reality of the referent is not a fact, *but* a problem . . . a problem of language.

7. The "only language" parapet leads us to another precaution. If "only language" is in charge of replacing the word 'being,' it should also correct one of its most serious implications: to speak about being is always taking a position in favor of the necessity or the contingency of being. Modern philosophy introduced the scientific principle of determinism. Even with its probabilistic limitations and the jigsaw puzzle of liberty, its omnipresence in language makes of any linguistic statement—be it literary, scientific, or common thought—a modal decision concerning a certain

quality of ontological necessity. "God exists" implies the necessity of the existence of God. "Yesterday I spoke with George" means that that conversation, even if unpredictable in its form, belongs to the facts that happened every day and are applications of a few physical laws. "I will come to see you tomorrow when I can" designates a hypothetical necessity, a commitment under conditions. Is the situation the same as when I say: "One uses the word 'cardinal' to designate a certain kind of bird"? Is the concept of *linguistic necessity* part of the concept of natural necessity or an independent concept qualifying some modes of being? My question is not to make an immediate decision concerning a basic epistemological problem in linguistics. I just know that, even when they reject the behaviorist or the physicalist patterns, linguists look for laws of language. Chomsky and his followers, for example, believe in the necessity of universal grammar, that is, the universal condition for any kind of historically possible tongues. They even suppose that one day their laws will be verified by brain physiology. Thus, in spite of themselves, mentalists rely upon a postponed physicalism, insofar as they keep the brain model in their intellectual background. They reserve for the future the physiological translation and confirmation of their present linguistic analyses. In any case, and at any time, the question of linguistic necessity—be it natural, cultural, or whatever it may be—stimulates their hypotheses and efforts at proof.

I am well aware that behind the present reflection on the concept of linguistic necessity, Hume's skepticism remains unanswerable, and the hypothesis of a duality between physical and human sciences is still open. Today, nobody would defend an epistemology of absolute determinism. However, discussions between subjectivists and objectivists in the interpretation of probabilities are still unsettled. No more settled, except if there is now a sort of respite, is the problem of the double aspect of language—psychological and sociological: which sort of determinism is dominant? If there is no possible reduction, how do psychology and sociology combine their laws? Those perplexities make and will make for many decades to come the bone of contention for linguists and philosophers of language.

There is still another and too often neglected question of the Leibnizian type: a historical language is a "possibility" that becomes "real" when many other possibilities were not selected. Then, ***a historical language is a "possible" that could not have been real***. With the theory of "compossibles," Leibniz hoped to save the absolute determinism of classical mechanism, and our modern probabilists committed themselves to the same enterprise of scientific rescue in refusing to consider this simple thought:

the diversity of known languages is the indirect proof that, although they are obviously what they are, they could have been different in very unpredictable ways. If, correcting Leibniz, one accepts the concept of "possible-impossible," or "possible-least possible," it does not mean that one is rejecting determinism in its general intention; one rejects the present and generally accepted idea of probabilist determinism: language is tacitly accepted as a necessary reality produced by a convergence of physiological, historical, cultural necessities. The fact that it could not have existed is ignored, which is not to say that it is contrary to the leading principles of sciences.

Such is my new caveat: *to meditate the idea of language as a "possible-impossible" is to cling to a vital intellectual life jacket.* I do not expect to eliminate the deterministic presupposition from the field of language and to make of linguistic events products of free creation, although such a poetic dream would be far from being absurd. I shall simply try never to forget that a word, a phrase, a sentence, obey a *contingent necessity,* that is, a necessity that, although radically unpredictable, is realizable. I do not forget that a Laplacean probabilist would tell me that my unpredictability is actually my ignorance: if all the interfering elements were "investigatable," I would realize that the word 'word' could not be other than it is in its phonetic, grammatical, and semantic characters. This may be, but the proof to be offered rests on Laplace's disciple. In the meanwhile I prefer to hold on to my life jacket. It is not because I received my language as a prefabricated product, protected by family and school, that I should consider it as an independent object with behaviors analogous to the predictable movements of the ocean. Language could have been completely different and it would have given me the same feeling of ineluctable evidence. I am not preaching in favor of radical relativism or skepticism. I issue, for my further meditation, a simple warning: *linguistic determinism, if it exists, is contained within a field of contingent possibles.*

Furthermore, attitudes toward linguistic determinism vary: they can go from passive acceptance or submission to controlled recognition or domination, and then, to transformism and invention. Such levels of linguistic experience depend upon our degrees of social participation and/or personal aptitudes. Considering the present state of linguistics, it seems to me sensible to restrain the temptation of scientific determinism, whatever it may be or become. The distinction between physical and linguistic determinism must stand, at least provisionally, without the implied reduction of one to the other. It is well known that physical necessity is first a product of our thought, and thus conceived through the qualification of our grammatical and semantic condition. Even if a reserved nominalist reduction would be naive and as arbitrary as physicalism can be, the pluralistic view of independent and interrelated determinisms deserves serious heed and, for the philosopher, it should be perceived as a flashing red light, allowing only very prudent transgressions.

To sum up, and to finish with this determinism caveat, let us say that, even when implicitly accepted by linguists in its vaguest and uncompromising generality, the determinism principle should be recognized as the most insidious source of epistemological entanglements. The philosopher, obsessively conscious of it, should bring himself or herself back again and again to the basic question of *language's awareness of its necessity*—a question leading to two codirections, that of the invention of its necessity, and that of the submission to it, with the possibility of many bypaths.

8. Risking intellectual paralysis by excessive cautiousness, am I not accumulating artificial reasons for vegetating indefinitely in the narthex of language reflection? Do the preceding caveats imply hidden linguistic pessimism? Curses against language are endemic and as frequent as its praise. Writers experience their writing as a permanent fight or personal vendetta. If Sartre felt that he had scores to settle with Flaubert, it was because, for him, Flaubert incarnated literature in itself. *The Idiot of the Family* cannot help hiding the pervasive bitterness of someone whose imperious need of writing felt continuously betrayed and never fully satisfied. Sartre's ultimate and paradoxical pessimistic humanism had its root in the progressive uneasiness of a worker who is loosing confidence, not in his gifts, but in the cherished tools of his cultural factory. This is one example among many. Does the love of language not entertain an unquenchable jealousy? Like the narrator of Proust's *The Prisoner,* any writer is sick of *ignoring* his language as well as his girl. Ignoring what? First, what is behind the unstransgressable signs; then, being conscious that, even at its extreme integrity, writing is always lying and deceiving: the veil of appearances is made of words. Maïa is language! Am I a trickster, a clown, or both?

I am uncovering another powerful implication in that deep-rooted, often unconscious, value judgment concerning my apprehension of writing. It oscillates between confidence and mistrust, love and hatred, exalted illusion and sarcastic blindness, linguistic optimism and pessimism. One or the other gives its personal marks to our rhythm and style. It radically modifies our comprehension of language. I am thus facing another caveat:

maybe it will be impossible to purify my awareness of language, of optimistic and pessimistic inclinations. Maybe such value judgments belong to the very moment language comes out of nothingness and bears its own weight of being. That remains to be discussed. In the meanwhile a sort of *critical wisdom* can be held to counterbalance and neutralize optimistic or pessimistic effects in the apprehension of language by itself, at least temporarily. Such a wisdom will consist in establishing oneself neither before nor after the consciousness of a linguistic Fall, at a point that is not yet the place for poetic benediction or moral malediction, for the positive or negative justification. It is not the renunciation of old age, the tired smile accepting an inevitable condition, the secret concession of the prisoner who ends up liking his jail. It is the wisdom that makes man capable of understanding the contingent fatality of his experience. It reaches its most intense expression in the awareness of arbitrary being, be it our own being or our own language. This is the unique mixing of the "already seen" and the "never seen," of repetition and novelty. At the level of philosophical heedfulness, it is the neutralization of the well-known to-and-fro of literary realism and nominalism, the double submission of language to reality and reality to language.

Indeed, I am well aware that by neutralizing a chronic epistemological difficulty, I have not solved it. I understand simply that my present intellectual state of affairs would lead my meditation nowhere. Wisdom is not a standstill after undecisive battles; it is the reorganization of beginnings for further cerebral reveries. In the literary field it has some kinship with the optimistic surrealist dream of "automatic writing"; but this time the writer-philosopher applies its wisdom to the fitness and appropriateness of the human brain in the practice of the abstract lexicon of a modern language. And, fringe benefit, we would be rid of the remnant belief in the existence of a perfect intellect that would live in a state of superior illumination if only it were not condemned to make of language its physical incarnation. Today such an illusion spares nobody, not even the mentalist Chomsky who becomes lyrical and trivial when he praises the infinite inventiveness of language. An easy-to-remember formula can condense the wisdom I aspire to; it should be muttered at least once a day, especially when one wakes up: *"everything, myself, the others, and the world, may we all do our best in the worst, unjustifiable, and inexcusable universe of words!"* That silent prayer could be called the lyrical sobriety of writing.

9. Now I would like to give a conclusion to my listing of preliminary caveats, underlining that, the critical wisdom I just recommended for

myself and others, to be more than just a nice way of speaking, should be at the core of our writing experience. More than once already, when not knowing what word to write to qualify my present "thinking" effort, I felt safe in calling for the word "experience" or its cognates, and implying that living language is experience and the reverse. Experience would be my personal safeconduct! Unfortunately, even though I had hoped to extricate myself from the "analogical field," I find myself in the middle of it: "experience" is just another easy metaphor with all sorts of slippery variations. However, its use cannot be helped.

Following Descartes, I proposed to call it 'meditation'; but I immediately understood that I could not follow Descartes imposing a quasi-mathematical order to his primitive words, which he calls innate ideas. Pascal's warning prohibits believing in the possibility of a primitive order of ideas and things. Meditation is condemned to live in the middle of its own disorder—a disorder that is not simply subjective: it reflects a state of mind inherited and implanted by education. Descartes knew it, but he was in a hurry and decided that one positive day of meditation would be enough to be radically rid of any kind of prejudices! On the contrary, I am conscious that meditation should be by itself a continuous and permanent fight against prejudices; and my first steps made me conscious, not of new and clean truths, but of caveats, that is to say, of the practical *cautiousness* that I will have to call back again and again in a sort of paradoxical continuity made of unsurpassable discontinuities. It means that each caveat should remain present in my mind at any time. I promise to review them, to call them back, to make them coexist and fight against the usual erosion of time and its power of oblivion.

In that perspective, if meditation is not an effort to put up basic words in a new order of words, it is no more an intimate diary or intellectual memoirs. As Husserl said, it is returning, not to the origin, but to the beginning of language as it is experienced at each moment of our personal history. I then realize that this return is definitive. I am condemned to stay, at that state, and that is the definite character of meditation in philosophical style: to search again and again for beginnings through the falsifications of current and organized languages. That justifies my present enumeration of caveats. It does not mean that I have overcome them and the prejudices they signal. Both of them stay omnipresent. That was probably Descartes' illusion, that writing against prejudices could eliminate them. That work is never ended; meditation is worse than Penelope's tapestry; everyday it starts again with the same tasks.

## *The Ambiguous Concept of Natural Languages*

It is well known that, since their beginnings at the end of the seventeenth century, the human sciences, sometimes called 'social sciences,' have been haunted by the antinomy "nature versus culture." Even when philosophers or scientists decided in favor of one or the other side, and declared themselves for a methodological naturalism or culturalism, they did not succeed in eliminating the other half of their option. Especially when the reference to nature is well inhibited, some values implied in its concept survive insidiously thanks to the surreptitious occurrence of the adjective 'natural.' The best instance of that situation is given by philosophers of language and linguists, who, openly or secretly, rely on the concept of "natural language," as opposed to "artificial language" and in synonymy with "common language." Here are a few revealing examples. In his *Cours de linguistique générale,* de Saussure sees in "langue," as opposed to "parole," "un tout en soi . . . un ordre naturel dans un ensemble" [language . . . speech . . . a whole in itself . . . a natural order in a group];[7] and in a very interesting comparison with the chess game, which later Wittgenstein will deepen, he observes that "une partie d'échecs est comme une réalisation artificielle de ce que la langue nous présente sous une forme naturelle" [a chess game is like an artificial realization of what language offers to us under a natural form].[8] The duality between nature and culture shows up when de Saussure defines 'literary language': "Par 'langue littéraire' nous entendons non seulement la langue de la littérature, mais, dans un sens plus général, toute espèce de langue cultivée, officielle ou non, au service de la communauté tout entière. Livrée à elle-même, (i.e., to its natural inclination), la langue ne connaît que des dialectes dont aucun n'empiète sur les autres, et par là elle est vouée à un fractionnement indéfini" [By 'literary language' we understand not only the language of literature, but in a more general sense, any kind of cultivated language, official or not, serving the whole community. Left to itself language comprehends dialects that do not encroach on one another, and consequently it is condemned to dispersion].[9] In 1972 Donald Davidson and Gilbert Hartman gave to a book they edited and devoted to the most important problems of contemporary philosophy of language the following title: *Semantics of Natural Languages.* In their introduction, they posit that linguistics is "treating natural languages as formal syntactic systems." Among the statements introducing his *Language and Linguistics,* John Lyons puts down that "the linguist is concerned primarily with natural language."[10] Sometimes the adjective 'natural' is replaced by 'ordinary,' for instance when Quine notes that "our ordinary language of physical things is about as basic as language gets," and warns us "not to treat ordinary language as sacrosanct."[11] Commendable advice indeed! But the meaning of 'ordinary' as substitute for 'natural' remains obscure. In the very different domain of poetry Stéphane Mallarmé identifies language with life itself and instinct: "A toute la nature apparenté et se rapprochant de l'organisme dépositaire de la vie, le MOT présente, dans ses voyelles et ses diphtongues, comme une chair; et dans ses consonnes, comme une ossature à disséquer" [Related to the whole of nature and similar to the organism in which life is deposited, the WORD, in its vowels and diphthongs, presents like a flesh and in its consonants like a bone structure to be dissected].[12]

Linguists who take a deliberate culturalist position do not avoid an implicit allusion to the natural power of language. In *Introduction à l'étude des langues indoeuropéennes,* Meillet, immediately stating that "la langue n'existe qu'en vertu de la société, de même que les sociétés humaines ne sauraient exister sans langues" [Language exists only in relation to society, for the same reason that human societies could not exist without languages], returns to a sort of sociological naturalism: "le système d'associations qu'est la langue ne se transmet pas directement d'individu à individu; comme on l'a dit, la langue n'est pas une oeuvre" [the associative system that is a language does not communicate itself from individual to individual; as it has been said, language is not a piece of work].[13] The Chomskian notion of "idealization" is nothing more than the projection of "natural language" into a mentalist perspective: "Linguistic theory is concerned primarily with an ideal speaker-listener, in a completely homogeneous speech-community, who knows his language perfectly and is unaffected by such grammatically irrelevant considerations as memory limitation. . . . This seems to me to have been the position of the founders of modern general linguistics, and no cogent reason for modifying it has been offered."[14] The "founders" to whom Chomsky refers were responsible for the pervasive concept of natural languages. One last example that proves that the concept of natural languages is still present in the most revolutionary thinking about the relation of language with perception, even as pure indexation: in *Vision* (1982) David Marr, discussing the problem of the "modularity" of systems, concludes that "natural language computer programs have contributed rather little to natural language understanding, with the recent exception of Marcus (1980) who has begun to construct a genuine two-level theory of the parsing algorithm we use."[15] If specialists know rather well what they mean when they speak of artificial intelligence, should we believe that, referring to 'natural language' they know more than what is present in a simple negative determination: 'natural language' is what is not 'artificial language'? Or must we make a slight change in the nominal syntagm 'natural language understanding' and read it 'language natural understanding' as opposed to 'language artificial understanding'? Later we will confront these problems. For the moment, we simply have to evaluate the semantics of an adjective heavily loaded by our philosophical traditions. This sampling could go on indefinitely.

My first reaction is to accept Lyons's comment: a biologist is constantly using the word 'life,' ignoring its metaphysical meaning but developing well-tested theories. Is not the linguist in a similar situation with the term 'language' and with the constant reference to 'natural languages'? However, the biologist never speaks of "natural life" except in the case of a certain type of life opposed to industrial or city life. When 'natural' is added to 'language,' strong implications are introduced that may not hamper present linguistic analyses but that could be damaging in the long run. At least, the legitimate unconcern of the linguists or the poets should not be accepted by philosophy. Semantic implications brought in by 'nature' and 'natural' should be clearly exposed before being declared innocuous.

It is easy to locate the beginning of modern semantics that have supported and continue to support three centuries of philosophical and scientific investigations. It was put into theoretical form by the great philosophers and mathematicians of the seventeenth century, Galileo, Descartes, Pascal, Leibniz, and Newton, who gave a new look to medieval theocentrism. Very soon the word 'nature' appeared to be a dangerous rival for 'God.' The famous Spinozist equation *Deus sive Natura* led to eighteenth-century naturalism. Pascalian pessimism concerning our fallen nature was apparently discarded. Leibniz was accused of being a hidden Spinozist and of identifying preestablished harmony with nature. Then, the concept of nature, as a term of universal reference for any kind of scientific research, became the strange marriage of *optimism and determinism.* Voltaire could laugh at Candide, but actually he invited his hero to convert himself into an optimist gardener. Rousseau helped add two more semantic marks to 'nature': *primitivity* and *instinct,* or *spontaneity,* or *creativity.* Nineteenth-century philosophers played powerful idealist, positivist, or realist symphonies based on those four key notes. Finally, who would claim that twentieth-century philosophers have not been impregnated with that semantic melody? Maybe 'consciousness' or 'culture' replaced 'nature,' which replaced 'God' in the modern role of lexical centrifugal power; but the four key notes can still be heard in Husserl's, Bergson's, Freud's compositions, or in the Hegelian-Marxist variations of our mid-century. Must we think, therefore, that the expression 'natural language' itself is completely freed from those overtones, independent of those philosophical implications, and that it has become pure designation empty of signification? Even if that were true, it would remain that, at the minimum of its negative determination, 'natural' qualifies 'language' as a product of 'nature'; and we find ourselves back with Voltaire and Rousseau, looking for the secrets of language in a preexisting Nature!

The conclusion seems to me obvious: we should *uncap* and thus neutralize any reference to a 'natural' property, or to 'nature' as cause of language processes. We should also avoid the expression 'natural language,' or any kind of substitute that could fill the empty place. Above all, the elimination of 'natural' should not serve the promotion of 'cultural' or 'artificial' and permit basic and vague generalizations such as "language is a product of human cultures," or "language, in its essence, even the so-called natural languages, is artificial." In the first case, no progress is made in the understanding of language: an unknown cause is presupposed: 'culture' is nothing less than God's proxy; or it is the occasion to introduce an entity that at the beginning of the twentieth century, linguists liked to invoke. For example, Michel Bréal, in *Essai de sémantique,* explains the evolution of language by human will, obscure, persevering, and collective: "Tout un peuple y collabore" [all of a people contributes to it].[16] Language is thus the emanation of "l'esprit populaire" ("popular spirit"). Later in the same essay, he speaks of a hidden intelligence.[17] The reference to collective psychology is significant: 'Nature' finds fashionable new alibis. These formulations express the same epistemological tendency toward explaining language by something else, of treating language as the effect of a cause identified with nature, and is vaguely reserved for future explorations. I absolutely reject that interpretation of language's natural causality, which seems to be omnipresent in contemporary linguistics as well as in philosophies of language: Such a proposition is neither evident nor proved; it requires justification. At the present state of meditation, it should be neutralized and not allowed to play the role of implied comprehension. In other words, let us say that *any basic qualification of language is dubious:* not only 'natural language' is to be eliminated from our vocabulary, but with it, its opposite components, such as 'cultural' and 'artificial.'

At its beginnings, the idea of natural language was associated with the eighteenth-century search for "general grammar" and "primitive language," as source of all historical languages. The problem of language was assimilated to the problem of its *origin*. Nineteenth-century linguistics's developments led to the conclusion that it was unscientific, not worthy of consideration. But it reappeared in a less naive form when Chomsky made a spectacular return to Cartesian syntax and innatism. Considering the complexity of this epistemological knot I should raise a new question: If the neutralization of the concept of natural language is an intellectual requirement, how can I approach the problem of its origin? Should I apply to 'origin' the interdictions put on the words 'nature' and 'culture'?

One can understand the methodological reserve of nineteenth-century linguists: turned toward the pasts of human cultures and languages, they can only observe developments with relative beginnings and ends; synchronies, as important as they can be for the understanding of languages, concern only momentary and artificial steps in the historical flow. However, without pretending to know what is, or not, accessible to linguistic observation, a meditation on the origin of language has a critical value for the philosopher in the effort to expose any kind of implication. Specialists—be they linguists or anthropologists—tell us that the concept of primitiveness when referred to Indo-European tongues or civilizations, is absurd: the *Rig Veda* crowns centuries of human history and at times, one feels that the origin is simply around us. Day after day, each human being, each society begins again the invention of its language and institutions; submission to tradition and learning techniques are just part of that continuous, creative effort. Adam and Eve play *today* the game of Paradise Lost. Thus, historical reflection by itself is a comparative game between past and present synchronies. Today, after centuries of social organization and administration, our "natural languages" have become well-protected institutions, codified common languages (in the sense that they belong to every citizen or member of such and such a society), on which specialized languages are grafted, be they literary, scientific, technological. The image of a tree of languages looks obvious: "natural languages" would be the roots that nourish any other linguistic creation. Maybe that metaphor is at the source of our modern belief in natural languages as primal objects of linguistic analysis: what we believed to be "natural" would actually be pure historical product. Is it not the well-known motto of contemporary culturalisms? If this is so, the notions of "natural" and "common" languages would be the result of socio-historical conditions, of social necessities of our modern ages, products of a progressive democratization of our societies: *languages belong to the people*.

From the moral point of view of our modern consciences such an attitude is commendable and, moreover, commonly accepted, even by those recurrent fascisms that dream of new aristocracies of violence, even by those aesthetic esoterisms that try to transform literary poetry and prose, painting, and sculpture into lofty hieroglyphs. Thus the synonymy "natural-common" thrives on in new terms: "popular" and "national." By universal right, language is the property of the people. Even the French Academy is supposed to speak and act on behalf of the French. Rivarol's contention that the French language is the perfect image of the "natural order" of thought is not dead. Such pretensions are not reserved to the French and their linguistic pride: similar ones make of each modern language a candidate for the expression of the universality of humankind.

Finally one discovers that 'natural' is hiding a very complex value—aesthetic, moral, and intellectual, in a unique cultural inspiration: the return to the origin is the conquest of a linguistic and cultural *naturalness;* and it is the ideal reflected in the elite's *usage*. It means that the elite speaks on behalf of itself as the ideal people. Such a phenomenon can take diverse forms and be experienced at diverse levels of a social group, in a given society. Different elites determine different usages, distinct natural languages in their specializations. In other words the so-called natural languages, far from being well-formed and unified systems, are composed of more or less codified usages with implicit or overt aristocracies that impose them. When descriptive linguistics claims to fix the practical rules of a given language, it confuses two linguistic conditions—a certain degradation of an ideal language into current practices, and traces of an ideal language as they succeed in surviving in spite of the daily entropy of usage. Thus, human tongues, as well as cultures, are made of compromises between entropy and order, between unpredictable solutions and too predictable ones, between a constant effort of recreation and the "least effort."

Up to now I have discussed the application of the expression 'natural languages' to our modern tongues, with the excuse that, if we are not linguists, at least we are the direct users of a few modern languages. What will happen if we try to apply our analysis to the hypothetic Indo-European as source of most of European languages? Once more we encounter the concept of naturalness. Meillet declares: "Tel est le type de l'évolution *spontanée*. Celle-ci résulte de la succession *naturelle* de générations, de l'emploi qui est fait du langage et de l'identitié de tendances et d'aptitudes que présentent les membres d'une suite de générations" [Such is the kind of *spontaneous* evolution; it results from the *natural* succession of generations, from the use which is made of language and from identical trends and aptitudes which the members of a series of generations offer].[18] Who would today believe in spontaneous or natural evolution, except in a very vague manner? When one listens to specialists of Indo-European and Sanskrit, one gets the strong feeling that the search for a natural state of language or for its cultural beginnings is pure fantasy, not only because such a state would be inaccessible to our observation, but, more significantly, because it has never existed. One can continue to speak about primitive or modern tongues, about barbaric and civilized tongues on behalf of Western cultural prejudices. Actually, at any moment of its morpho-semantic expression, each language is totality and perfection, awareness of control over brute matter, as if any kind of language felt itself "sanskrata" (achieved, completed, perfect, per se, autarky), as if Sanskrit were the model to return to in order to understand ancient and modern tongues. The history of linguistics since the beginning of the nineteenth century could be written from that perspective. If one looks, not at the attempt to reconstruct a basic Indo-European language, but, with Louis Renou for instance, at Sanskrit in its most ancient Vedic forms, one is faced with the implicit duality of a known and written literary language as privileged expression of a great civilization, and an unknown language spoken by the people. Then one supposes that the former is a miraculous excrescence of the latter, in the same way as we think that our literature grows and blooms above the soil of our common tongues.

Nothing is less certain. Is the reverse hypothesis so absurd? Why not consider the so-called common or natural languages as surpassed forms of language, and look for the essence of languages in their literary quest for perfection? This explains my decision not to take artificial examples drawn from an imaginary common usage ridiculed by Ionesco.

What does 'literary' mean? Is it the search for perfection, for a unique totalization? Is it the desire of ultimate formula or supreme expression in the form of principles? If so, Vedic hymns would represent language in its absolute incorporation of *language principle* as *language religion*. Benveniste's comments on "religion" in *Indo-European Language and Society* deserve our attention: The Indo-European language, he says, had no term to designate religion as a separate institution. Would this be because religion was the totality of human experience and thus language itself? One may read also the Vedic hymn "Speech": "I [Speech] am the one who says, by myself, what gives joy to gods and men. Whom I love I make awesome, I make him a sage, a wise man, a Brahmin"[19] and with the same title, in Louis Renou's *Hymnes spéculatifs du Véda,* a poem where speech and sacrifice are assimilated:

> Grâce au sacrifice, ils ont marché dans les sentiers de la Parole,
> ils l'ont découverte comme elle était entrée chez les poètes.
> Quand les Sages [the Poets Seers] purifiant leur pensée comme la farine
> par le crible, créant la Parole à l'aide de la pensée . . .
>
> [Thanks to sacrifice, they have walked on the paths of the Word,
> they have discovered it as it had entered the poet's world.
> When the Wise Men purifying their thoughts like flower
> with a sieve, creating the Word with the help of thought . . .][20]

Religious life is the life of speech, creating at the same time cosmos and poem. However, coming back to Benveniste's study on etymological analysis, we can note that in Latin, *religio* comes from *relegere,* which means to collect again, to take up again for a new choice, to return to a previous synthesis in order to recompose. Later, Christians will connect *religio* with *religere* (to tie) and see in religion an objective bond between the believer and God. There we are, far from the earlier praise of Speech and the admiration of its thaumaturgic powers, but the belief in the religious nature and function of language is not lost.

To these fragmentary remarks one may object that if the connection between language and religion is indispensable and even too obvious, it does not imply that language *as* religion is the source of all other possible languages, the common language of communication. Let us turn to Dumézil's well-known theory on the Indo-European gods. He classifies them in three groups corresponding to three social classes covering entirely human activities—priests, warriors, clans of shepherds. Each group takes care of one of the three essential functions: administration of the world in its mysterious and regular way, games of physical strength including the actions of war, wellfare of society. Should we conclude that this tripartite division implies a similar linguistic distribution: language of religion, language of power and war, language of economy? Such a distinction is likely. One can even find indirect proofs of it when reading French humanists of the sixteenth century. For example, Henri Estienne condemns the French courtiers who borrowed from Italy their war vocabulary, as if French warfare depended upon the Italian school. In a similar spirit, Etienne Pasquier in "Quelle est la vraie naïveté de notre langue et en quels lieux il la faut chercher" [What is the real originality of our tongue and where one should look for it] proposes to enrich vernacular French with the help of the very expressive languages of all sorts of craftsmen. Awareness of the presence of multiple dialects in France is striking as is the need for a common language surpassing, although benefiting from, local and particular dialects, even aspiring to what the eighteenth century will call "universal language" with its "natural" grammar and codes imposed on the people by the Court and the Academy.

Shall we draw the conclusion that "common" languages emerge from the stuff of particular tongues that are actually composed of a common syntax with phonetic variations and specialized lexicons and semantics? Anthropology and history show us another and very significant fact: "common" languages presuppose the collective consciousness of a group, a consciousness incarnated in a dominant subgroup—the Church, the Court, with individual persons speaking on their behalf, especially poet-priests, court poets, or humanists, who are true masters and disseminators of languages. Does this mean that common languages, in their regional universality, are under the control of small and powerful groups, and finally, among these groups, under the control of a few "authorities," that is, individuals recognized as such? A well-known debate indeed, which has taken many forms since the birth of human sciences! It is also responsible for the diversification and overlapping of those sciences under the label of human or social sciences. One will notice that the study of language reflects the same pluralistic image. Maybe the expression 'natural,' or 'common,' language has today become a convenient, hypothetical, general ground for all those researchers, each trying hard to absorb the others in his or her own system, all of them constructing a scientific Babel. But what can a philosopher make of this state of cultural affairs?

It is time to complete our critical examination of the field around the concept of "natural language"; I shall thus establish the list of notions to be uncapped and neutralized. By and large, those notions form the loose semantic system constituting the background of human sciences since the end of the eighteenth century. First culprit, the antinomy "nature/culture." Then, swarming around it, "culture and history," "society versus person," "social levels and interferences," "religion and poetry," "contemplation and action," "model and inertia," "invention and imitation," "physical and spiritual powers," and so on. Such an enumeration could be endless. I do not question the convenience and efficacy of any of those semantic oppositions for this or that epistemological purpose, and I understand very well that without them there would be no human sciences, the latter seeming to be governed by the wise rule: something is better than nothing! However, that rule does not apply in philosophy, especially in philosophy of language. Do we have to conclude that semantic skepticism should be the ultimate destination of philosophy, which, in our time, has to stay on the curb, furiously crying or smiling with desabused tolerance at the heavy traffic on the highways of scientific knowledge? Not necessarily! Conceptual neutralization does not mean radical intellectual destruction, not even referential suspension, Husserlian style. Simply, but sharply, it is an *exposition of implications,* that is, an empirical awareness of what I presuppose each time I raise a problem, choose a method, or offer a solution. The language of exposition does not claim to forbid anything. It pays painstaking attention to linguistic automatisms and to their inertia. That sort of philosophical contemplation does not designate a psychological state of consciousness, simply the linguistic intelligence of caveats. Caveats do not form a system of principles, but rather a *coexistence of warnings.* As I have indulged in traffic metaphors, let us say that they do not play the role of stop signs; they are yellow flashes indicating "proceed with care." The function of the philosopher is not to let them in a state of insidious presentiment but to embody them in a neat formulation.

## *Listing Caveats*

*First caveat:* It would be naive to advise the radical elimination of the syntagm 'natural language.' Again and again it reappears as disguised synonymies or approximations like 'common,' 'universal,' 'national,' and so on. Furthermore the passage is too easy from "natural language" to "nature of language," or to "essence of language." I am cautious with the adjective 'essential.' There is still the possibility of the reverse formulation "language of nature," as if nature was a product of language, a certain way of speaking. Finally I advise suspicion with a sentence like this, "One of the happiest trends in philosophy in the last twenty years has been its naturalization."[21]

*Second caveat:* it is similar to the first one but applied to the word 'culture.' The situation is even more treacherous because when referring to culture one hopes to avoid the trap of naturalism. It is only a transfer to another kind of phrasing. Let us realize that the sentence, "Language is a product of culture," if not meaningless, constitutes improductive tautology and reversibility. Saying that, I add nothing to my former vague understanding about culture; I am just a little more confused.

*Third caveat:* this time, it concerns 'history,' with similar kinds of impotent identities and the permanent temptation of reversibility between "history is language," "language is history," and "language of history is the history of language." I am aware (it is part of the caveat) that, as a philosopher, I cannot live without using those expressions. At least I should know or keep remembering that they are not simple or innocent. By the same token, playing with those words, independently or simultaneously, I am warned that the methodological passage from simple ideas to complex ideas is a typically philosophical illusion of inference.

*Fourth caveat:* the concept of "spirit of language" and its subsequent incarnations have the same slippery quality as the preceding ones. It is immediately present as soon as I write the simple "language is. . . ." It is as if I were conferring upon language a causal power the modes of which I do not know, modes often vaguely implying the physical model of *natural* sciences, a linear, structural, mechanical, or statistical model. At the minimum of neutralization, I can entertain the two following doubts: *is the concept of causality applicable to language*? And if so, do today's tested scientific models or the traditional philosophical ones offer the possibility of a linguistic translation and understanding? Those hypotheses, although commonly accepted, are less than probable. "Language of causality" does not necessarily imply "causality of language." It is not absurd to consider 'causality' as a creation of language and, as such, not applicable to its creator. We are back to the initial question of our meditation, *"Is language applicable to language?"* What do we mean when we confer upon language the quality of reflecting-designating itself, or treating itself as subject-object of reference? How can one speak of "language of language"? Is it the 'nature' or 'spirit' of language? It is obvious that that question destroys itself and changes language into a "something else."

*Fifth caveat:* Let us call it the *grammatical* caveat that is well known by Western philosophers, who since Plato and the sophists have meditated on ontologico-grammatical parallelism. As soon as I write, "What is *x*?," I introduce a causal system and with it, the belief in a divine, natural, or cultural *order,* innate or acquired. Chomsky sees in the relation between nouns and verbs the basic competence of language, implying that this relation is biologically founded. Therefore his innatism is very relative. It is currently accepted that our brain is the product of an evolution. Does that mean that the human brain is a product of learning? A question with no possible answer! Even if an answer were possible, it could not help to solve the problem of understanding language as an order of a certain kind, reducible or not to an already known order. All philosophical *-isms* are patent techniques of reducing coexisting orders to a supposedly dominant order—be it called God, Nature, Culture, or Language itself. When I state that language is the way to obtain the total expression of Being through the divine, natural, or cultural Order, I am giving sense to the language of Being through the language of God, the language of Nature, the language of Culture. Then, I suppose the transparency of language; I behave as if I needed to forget the existence of language in order to think the existence of Being. I suppose an invisible order to make God, Nature, and Culture visible.

My exercise in semantic exposition could go on indefinitely. More *caveats* could be added, because each linguistic moment would require its own. As we have already seen, meditation cannot benefit from the accumulating progress of knowledge, which makes of sciences the totalization described by Pascal as the growing-up of a unique Man who becomes taller and bigger from generation to generation. Meditation is an effort of transversal possession or, better, of recuperation, establishing a minimal order that is just consciousness of possible disorders, pure fight against disorders remaining to be identified. Then, without too much pretense, the philosopher may wonder if, in his intense meditating standstill he does not reach the zero-moment of language expression, in the same way as the poet hopes to find the perfect ellipsis, when lexical and syntactic distinctions are abolished, when there are only promises of names and verbs, promises of interrogation, exclamation, and declaration. Before the progress of technological and scientific languages, before the fallout of common languages, before all the possible, natural, or cultural orders, and with the complicity of poetry and, more generally, of literary genres, the philosopher rediscovers language in its hesitations between order and disorder, sense and nonsense.

A very disappointing conclusion indeed! After all these circles around the central problem of language, do we arrive at the decision to look for a theory of sense? Surely the philosopher needs one more caveat: *beware of synonyms*! Today's theories of sense or meaning form the most impressive intellectual jungle one can imagine. I will have to decide later if I am able to find my way through it. Meanwhile, I can voluntarily stay stuck with my minimal perception of language as struggle against any kind of disorder and identify that insight with the consciousness of meaning: "giving sense" meaning refusing felt disorder. However, the act of meditation, as described above, should not be concerned with meaning as understood by the so-called man on the street nor by the scientist and his or her technological followers; that is, with a hypothetical state of language independent of its physio-sociological origin and of its objects of reference.

Meditation also rejects Austin's duality between the constative and performative functions of language. For the philosopher, and contrary to the linguist, those functions are indissociable and felt in a unique experience of performing sense in its creative power. The being of meditation is identical to the being of meaning and to the meaning of being. It is the experience of *becoming other than one is,* and also of *being in a state of reference.* I am not yet ready to grapple with the problem of the relation of reference and sense and to explore Frege's famous articles on this matter. I am just conscious of my own present writing as a living experience that, through its multiple warnings and caveats makes me more aware of language as a secret alliance between internal order and reference.

Let us emphasize that meditation is not a psychological operation, but a special act of writing and of making myself exist as writer. It is language *on* language made possible by language *of* language where the same is the other and in reverse, the other the same. Thus my own conscious existence depends not on the pure act of my writing about my writing but on the act as referential power: I refer to myself writing about writing. In his second *Meditation,* "De la nature de l'esprit humain et qu'il est plus aisé à connaître que le corps," Descartes quickly disposes of the threat of skeptical paralysis thanks to a sort of existential coup d'état. Out of his act of writing, he makes the sentence "I think, therefore I am" and the declaration of its necessary truth, as clear and distinct intuition, the unsurpassable and absolute evidence of reference. Husserl had his own doubts about such certitude, but, not really leaving the psychological level, he was himself too hasty in establishing the intersubjectivity of the *Cogito.* In brief, on behalf of a very hypothetical language transparency, Cartesian and Husserlian evidence hide and justify the obscure operation of reference as transparence transposed into intellectual achievement. Thus, if we take back philosophical language to the transversal ups and downs of meditation and, for our own benefit, begin again the linguistic experience of Descartes or of Husserl, it becomes clear that our subject-object of meditation is not Being or Consciousness, the interrelation of the Self, the World, and God, but the *unique experience of reference* in any of the multiple manifestations that mark language's appearances.

As a result, our caveats will not remain general warnings without specific purpose. Their role is to protect the *access to reference* and, returning to our introductory metaphor, to authorize our decision to leave the narthex for the cathedral of language and its public or private services. Then, with one certitude only in the chaos of semantic implications and virtualities, the *experience of reference* emerges not as the experience absorbing any other linguistic processes but as the *irreducible problem*.

One last attempt at more consciousness, that is, at more writing on what has already been written: Meditation is taking hold of itself once more, in the form of interrelated caveats. It experiences reason, not because of epistemological doubts but out of cautiousness; it is an *exercise in suspicion* and, as such, it is tense work of language on language. Analytical philosophy puts itself in the strange situation of accepting natural languages in their "natural" expressions and of practically rejecting their philosophical systematizations as nonsensical. It was repeating the old dream of language before the Fall and its philosophical perversions—a sort of naturalistic optimism converted into theoretical pessimism. Our "wisdom" sees no reason for being one or the other, or to end with a skeptic and ironic compromise. It nurtures a single hope, but with no self-assurance: to be able to go beyond the present culture of caveats, looking for their secret coherence and deep raison d'être. We are aware of two dominant and imperative conditions: (1) There is no language without *power of reference* and thus, without a language of reference and its multiple rulings. Meditation's next step should lead to their evaluation; (2) The processing of attention in meditation faces a peculiar situation, which I call *consciousness of implications*. Most of the recognized caveats are diverse aspects of that consciousness and parts of a *language of implications* that constitutes a feeling of *clair-obscur* for any linguistic performance. From now on our attention will focus on 'reference' and 'implication,' with the understanding that those terms are susceptible of being the object of meditation through a language. I speak of reference, of implications, or I write about them. Thus, the new principal questions are the following: *How is a language of reference possible? How is a language of implications justified?*

## *Preparing Meditation for Its New Exercises*

Not knowing the hows and whys, I am conscious that I exist and that language exists. It is too early to write, "I think, I know that . . . " I just write two propositions: "I exist, language exists." I can join them and make of them a single statement: "I exist in language by the very act of writing. Language exists in me by my writing," implying that the reversed phrasings are equivalent . . . but in what way? Does the relation between me and language express a deep necessity or is it pure coincidence? It is impossible to decide. I take it as a double *coexistence,* a fact that I am unable to bypass or forget, a fact to which I have already given a name: meditation, as qualifying the act thanks to which I and language come to existence with one stride. Descartes was victim of the "haste" *(précipitation)* that he had denounced as one of the two capital sins of intellectual life (the other one being prejudice): he attributed to language three basic referents—I (as human spirit), God, and the World, thus giving to meditation the duty of qualifying language's principal domains of reference. Doing so, he more or less gave to more than three centuries of human understanding its chart for new explorations and experimentations; but, obsessed by the remapping of referents, he forgot, and many after him, to meditate on reference itself; simply he forgot he was writing "I think." Instead of returning constantly to language, as Montaigne did in his *Essais,* Descartes lost himself into the translucent world of knowledge with the three basic concepts of *representation, mind,* and *function,* which for the Western modern cultures, served to determine the conditions of reference. These concepts themselves mark the *double impossibility of thinking about language without establishing a relation to something else and of thinking about something else without the presence of language.*

Meditating on this dualistic state of reference, Western philosophy and especially epistemology, opened after Descartes an intellectual battleground around three propositions that I propose to call respectively the *realist,* the *spiritualist,* and the *instrumentalist* conditions, and which I formulate in the following way: (1) *there is no language without an external referent;* (2) *there is no language without an internal referent;* (3) *there is no language without the understanding of itself as a function.* Needless to say, each of these conditions has been source of philosophical systematizations in our modern culture, as if philosophy's main, but secret, charge has been the continuous theory of language as power of reference and expression of truth. The first two conditions were contrasted under the labels of *realism* and *idealism.* The antinomic pair *materialism/spiritualism* was at times added to radicalize the opposition in very complicated manners: Whatever those philosophical differentiations may have been, they always imply the double independence of subject and object of language, with the help of the omnipresent duality of exterior/interior. Although latent since the early Greek beginnings of reflection on the nature of language, the third condition waited until the second part of the nineteenth century to find its opened philosophical expression and again with a divergent movement toward realism or idealism: realist as well as idealist instrumentalisms were proposed, the best examples being European *Marxism* and American *pragmatism*.

It would be contrary to the spirit of the present meditation to write another philosophical tale from the point of view of the theory of language, even if there is today an obvious need for rewriting the histories of Western and Eastern philosophies as the understandings and justifications of language without language, or with language in the footnotes. I just hope that those comments will invite historians to give to explicit or implicit theories of language their central place in the totalizing efforts of philosophers, although most of the time they feigned to believe in the transparency of language and relegated their thoughts on language proper in the margins of their investigations on being and mind. For the moment, I shall try to trace a few paths through the philosophical jungle, remaining aware that my consciousness of language depends upon the understanding and experience of reference, and prepared by a few caveats which, I repeat, are not strict imperatives at the beginning of a philosophical research, but caution signs in the use of implicit concepts such as "naturalness" of language, linguistic contingencies, and determinisms, and their very tricky implication. It is now time to proceed, and to meditate on the first condition of reference, knowing that this new phase is not a real progress as compared to the first meditation. I shall return more than once to the warnings of which I became conscious, and I shall maintain that way of thinking-writing, which following Descartes, I called *meditation* out of philosophical obligation. After many approximations, and before grappling with the basic conditions of language through the experience of reference, I come to a last formulation: *to meditate is to make language aware of itself as language,* that is, never to forget that, when I write, I am writing; doing so, my writing is losing its normal function of affirming and negating values; for instance, it cannot pretend to be true or to denounce falsities. Descartes, attempting to transpose the multiple writings of Montaigne's *Essais,* did not realize that he could not transcend language itself and that he could not convert a pluralistic writing into a unilinear demonstration. Thus, meditation properly conducted can only *uncap* the values immanent to language. *Uncapping* does not designate an epistemological metaphor; it aims at a real experience in writing. I cannot properly describe it; I can only ask my reader to become conscious of it when, with me, he or she relives the *referring condition*.

# MEDITATION TWO

# *Uncapping the Realist Condition and Its Philosophies*

## *Varieties of Realism*

As a precaution, I shall avoid a direct confrontation with the *concept of reality*. I shall deal with it only indirectly, insofar as it appears in that understanding of languages that centuries of Western philosophies have called "realisms." In the current usage of the term 'realism' there are four main categories of realism, even if in each case, definitions vary widely: *naive realism*, or realism of common sense, *scientific realism*, *philosophical realism*, and *artistic realism*. The first two just imply or affirm that representation represents something independent of itself—the only, although important, difference being that for science true representation of reality radically differs from the so-called naive perception of things. In our meditation both will play the role of *witnesses;* they do not claim that they are drawing conclusions about the ultimate essence of knowledge, or about the universe and language. Artistic realism, as histories of literature and of art refer to it, is very elusive. It is based on the aesthetic principle that art, whatever it may be, must express reality as it is perceived or felt, not as it could be beautified by our imagination. It is based upon naive realism and on certain rules of expression, so that often artistic realist expressions appear to be the opposite of reality perceived; it is true construction of reality. Sometimes it is termed 'magic' or 'poetic': for example, Flaubert, Mallarmé, Céline can be considered as interesting witnesses in our meditation, but not as realist theoreticians of language. Thus, the third category, that of philosophical realism, seems to be our main target. In spite of their diverse and at times contradictory qualifications, all realisms, as we know them through the history of philosophy or in our present cultures, posit two general statements: "Being as referent exists outside knowledge, which is part of it," and "Being in itself is not basically modified by knowledge, which is on the contrary modified by it." From here, there are as many realisms as there are philosophers who proclaim they are realist.

## *Naturalist Inclinations*

Attempting to trace the subtleties of those theoretical differences would be exhausting and finally, useless. Through the present-day intellectual confusion around the realist creed, two attitudes tend to be generally accepted: (1) realism is actually a *naturalism:* its epistemological principles are rooted in the belief in the existence of a human nature having innate or acquired values; (2) the knowledge of external objects presupposes observations and depends on sensory stimulations; the most abstract scientific statements always return to observational data.

P. F. Strawson in *Skepticism and Naturalism: Some Varieties* gives a typical example of this "new" realism, a mixture of naturalism and scientism, an advocacy of the great principles of the Enlightment, an effort to surpass the Kantian epistemological duality of empirical realism and transcendental idealism, a claim to rewrite a modernist version of Humean skepticism and to formulate a new agnosticism behind our cultural values. The connivance with the concept of 'natural language' is as obvious today as it was yesterday: realism finds its justification in the belief in human nature and its sensorial condition. The striking success of 'natural sciences' brings a posteriori proof of the naturalistic and empirist beliefs.

Realism can be understood as the *imperative of concreteness* and the effort to get an efficient language, a true mimesis, not of a Platonic ideal world, but of the perceived physical world. One may concur with Mario Understeiner's interpretation of the Greek sophistic culture in *I Sofisti* (1949): sophists did not lead toward skepticism, contrary to Plato and Aristotle's accusations, but toward realism and phenomenalism. The sophist view of the world is that of reality as tragic, ironic, and unsurpassable contradiction. Outrageous paradoxes expose the impossibility of a coherent language for space, time, and more generally, for syntactic order; the most important of them, the well-known *sophism of the Liar* shows the contrast between direct and reflective discourses; and all of them concern the immanent contradiction of language within its own constitution. Actually, they implicitly refer to and are the consequences of the realist condition: they play on the impossibility of establishing a correspondence between language and reality as independent from each other. Belief in reality, then, is represented as stronger than any skeptical conclusion; it is an instinct that makes the skeptic climb a tree to escape from a barking dog! Thus, reality is the *irrational* that resists the efforts of language in keeping the world in its conceptual nets. In modern thought, at least, for those philosophers who rejoin the sophistic current, "irrational" takes different forms. Often it designates the irreducible 'particular.' Such is the paradox formulated by John Locke in the *Essay on Human Understanding:* there is a gap between the generality of language and the particularities of things, that is, between abstraction of concepts and particularity of things as felt by sensory experience. The modern idea of "unknowable" and the diverse modern expressions of agnosticism also appear: an unknowable reality is supposed to exist before it is felt as particular beings in sensations that are later elaborated into general ideas.

Reality, understood as a state independent of language, is posited as a necessity. Then discussions of its nature are open to interpretation: is it a logical or natural necessity, that is, a theoretical or practical necessity? It depends upon the philosophical conceptions of logical or natural order. Belief in reality can be felt as evidence, postulate, absolute language condition, and in a way, life condition: be a realist or commit suicide! Is this the last word of realism?

## *Internal Realism*

Let us continue our inquiry among contemporary confessed realists. John R. Searle, making fun of Jacques Derrida in his review of John Culler's *On Deconstruction: Theory and Criticism after Structuralism* laughs at any attempt to reduce "reality" to language: "it seems positively exhilarating to be told that what we call 'reality' is just more textuality."[1] More convincingly, in *Intentionality, an Essay in the Philosophy of the Mind* (1983), Searle neatly and strongly declares that:

> Realism is part of the Background in the following sense. My commitment to "realism" is exhibited by the fact that I live the way I do, I drive my car, I drink my beer, write my articles. . . . This is not to say that realism is a true hypothesis, rather it is to say that it is not a hypothesis at all, but the precondition of having hypotheses."[2]

What does Searle call "background"? "[It] is a set of nonrepresentational capacities that enables all representing to take place" (p. 143). One is not surprised when, later in his analysis, he qualifies his defense of realism as "naturalistic." He accepts Frege's theory on reference and meaning from the point of view of "a kind of biological naturalism": "intentionality is a biological phenomenon and it is part of the natural world like any other biological phenomenon" (p. 230). In his epilogue on "The Intentionality and the Brain" he reaffirms this biological naturalism: "Like these other phenomena [as, lactation, digestion] mental states are caused by biological phenomena and in turn cause other biological phenomena."(p. 264).

We come back to the story of the skeptic in a tree, but a skeptic who believes in the existence of "mental" states and calls himself *internalist* in the sense that "it is in virtue of some mental states in the head of a speaker or hearer . . . that they can understand linguistic references" (p. 198). The discussion of internalism should be reserved for future meditations because one can catch Searle transferring his realism into other philosophical options. Finally, is his "intentionality" far from Derrida's "textuality"? One may wonder. In any case, he gives us a good example of the modern circular games one can play with the word 'nature,' founding science on behalf of scientific truths, and with the duality exterior/interior: exterior things are interior to intentional thinking and acting. Searle could call himself a biological idealist as well, or, secretly, a Husserlian who is deliberately ignorant of the implications of his own assumptions.

A true realist should be anti-internalist, if he sincerely believes in the radical independence of reality from thought-and-language. (I shall not discuss now their own and reciprocal independence); and he would accept Hilary Putnam's provocative statement "Meanings are not in the head," a statement that implies all the more that things are not in the head, but in nature, which includes human minds. However, following Putnam from his *Mind, Language and Reality* (1975) to his *Realism and Reason* (1983), one can only be puzzled. If he rejects intentionality as "a power which enables to refer" he tries to define in his terms a sort of *internalism,* strictly opposed to the verificationism of Logical Positivism.[3] In his preface to *Reason, Truth and History* he describes his book as an effort to escape the dichotomy objectivity/subjectivity and to go back to Kant's ideas. Putnam observes that "Kant proposed for the first time an internalist view of truth," he is an "internal realist" (p. 60). Truth is based on rationality; it is "an *idealization* of rational acceptability" (p. 48); it is "ultimate goodness of fit" (p. 64); finally, it belongs to "our rational nature" (p. 60). With such statements, are we far from Searle's biological naturalism? We get more precision in Putnam's *Realism and Reason:* he proposes a human kind of realism for which truth is an "idealized justification." After recognizing that realism is "the central dispute in the philosophy of language" (p. 1), he offers a critical review of contemporary theories of reference, and in his concluding pages he again pays homage to Kant's defending a kind of "property dualism we are committed to": "It is the kind of dualism Kant acknowledged"; we are not able to overcome what Kant called the "dualism of experience" (p. 302). Thus, internalist realism is a relativist, anthropocentrist rationalism, which is a naturalism, which is the empirical dualism of subjectivity and objectivity, without which language could not exist and human life would be impossible.

Does this mean that those philosophers and many others—whatever their differences may be—are dreaming of a new Enlightenment for the year 2000, a new humanism adjusted to the progress of science from Newton's natural philosophy to the philosophy of the computer age? From the point of view of a realist of strict obedience, these new perspectives are just hidden, bashful idealisms that elude the realist challenge as it was expressed by Etienne Gilson in *Le Réalisme méthodique:*

> Or l'idéalisme, du fait qu'il va de la pensée aux choses, ne peut savoir si ce dont il part correspond ou non à un objet; lorsqu'il demande au réaliste comment rejoindre l'objet en partant de la pensée, ce dernier doit donc s'empresser de répondre qu'on ne le peut pas, et que c'est même la principale raison pour ne pas être idéaliste, car le réaliste part de la connaissance, c'est-à-dire d'un acte de l'intellect qui consiste essentiellement à saisir un objet.
>
> [Idealism, because it goes from thoughts to things, cannot know whether that from which it starts corresponds or not to an object; when it asks the realist how to join the object when starting from the thought, the latter must then hasten to answer that it is impossible, and that is even the main reason for not being an idealist, because the realist starts from knowledge, that is, from an act of the intellect that consists of grasping an object.][4]

For the faithful Thomist Gilson, a coherent realist should not commit himself to Kant's transcendental idealism! Furthermore, the transfer of the realist belief to a biological law acknowledging the dualities of experience solves nothing. It comes down to confessing that I cannot think and live without accepting the duality of subject and object: I perceive and act within its limits. Then, why not go a little further, rejoining and radicalizing analytical philosophy? Philosophical ways of raising problems are senseless and useless; let us forget them and wait for science's achievements, not even claiming to correct language, leaving linguists to do their jobs, even if today the results are disappointing. In other words, philosophy should be language put to silence.

We know the answer to that invitation: the talking of philosophers cannot be stopped without stopping any other kind of language. "Realism" is a dominant part of that linguistic condition. However, even with new realism, whatever its adjectives may be, the dogma of old realism remains present: behind the "dualities of experience" lies unelaborated the belief in the substantial duality between language and reality. I do not see any experience or reasoning that can justify it. It is a sort of ontologized *coup de force*. Philosophers of the realist creed repeat again and again that one cannot live or think without its acceptance. Of that I am less than certain. I am afraid that *philosophical realism is an aspect of artistic realism*.

As a consequence, I should revise my first conclusion: the need for realistic positions is shared by all kinds of users, be they philosophers, scientists, novelists, or painters. Thus, "reality" is understood not as a fact but as a *value* applied to language itself. There are realist techniques of language thanks to which language is said to be expressing reality or, as is often said, *referring to reality*. It is not surprising that today philosophies of knowledge have become philosophies of language, which in their turn put at their center the problem of reference. I can only conclude that 'reality' would find its place within a meditation (I am not speaking of theory) on reference; and there is no need for the intervention of pseudoscientific generalities, with Darwinian or Lamarkian overtones, concerning our lifestyle, our thought, or action. If the meditation on language and reference must come first, there is no reason why naturalistic implications should be called upon for help, nor why a paradoxical kind of realist prelanguage be slipped under "natural" languages. Gilson is clearer but equally inoperative when he subordinates his linguistic realist rulings to a metaphysical language of knowledge. The substitution of the word 'nature' for the word 'God' did not help the sciences become conscious of their own languages.

The hypothesis of a *realist prelanguage* cannot be discarded too lightly with the easy accusation of being a vicious circle. It could be said, and actually has been said, that the circular nature of languages is a normal condition and that we should learn to live with it. This way of behaving is well known today under the name of *hermeneutics,* its most illustrious representative being Martin Heidegger.

### *Heidegger's Dasein*

Whereas Anglo-Saxon neorealism makes a clear return to Kant whose basic epistemological patterns gave to its diverse proponents the safety of an independent referent and the satisfaction of a description of mental activities, Heidegger takes Kant as the perfect counterexample, the last great representative of Western ontology, the Aristotle of the modern age. Heidegger is right: the famous critical problems "How is mathematics possible? How is physics possible? Is Metaphysics possible?" do not change the fundamental Parmenidian question: "What is Being?" By introducing epistemology Kant was exposing a new version of the knowledge of Being, not a new version of Being. The new methodology of mathematical physics brought a new language to be grafted onto the old. On the other hand, Heidegger understands that the problematic of Being must be radically transformed. The question, "What is Being?" already implies the solution of an independent referent, which is there to be known. The Parmenidian ontological question, which is a pure vicious circle between noun and verb, requires hermeneutic translation; it takes the form, "What does Being signify?" However, such a formula remains close to the old question and implies a basic duality of noun and verb, as if the change of verb ('to signify' instead of 'to be') were not changing the required independence of the referent. This is why Heidegger finds a better way of expressing the hermeneutic problem: "How is the understanding-of-being possible?"

In *The Basic Problems of Phenomenology* he even suggests another way of writing it: "How can something immanent in consciousness refer to something transcendant out there in the objects?"[5] It is a hopeless situation with only one exit: reflecting on what would be the subject inside which something-like-being-true is supposed to have its own existence. Metaphors of *unveiling, disclosure, opening up* permit an "understanding" of the transference from the subject to the object . . . but within the subject. At the same time, it is the truth and the reality of Being as being-there—the introduction of the *Dasein,* subject and object of the preontological understanding of Being, the fundamental experience of existence, not only the experience of being there (*da*) but that of "to be the there." I would say, in an Heideggerian spirit, that the *Dasein,* as the understanding-of-being, is the power of understandness in its universal qualification. As such it has no essence; it is not conceptualizable; it is transcendency as intentional being projecting the world; it is perception as uncoveredness of things in its highest generality. Thus 'Dasein' does not signify "Whatness" but "whoness" or the "praesens" of a general quality. For example, the hammer and its hammering presuppose a general intention of hammerhood. It is just the same for the world, first existing in its worldhood.[6]

Reserving for further meditation Heidegger's conception of sense and reference, let us limit ourselves to the question, is the Heideggerian philosophy of the *Dasein* a metaphysical interpretation of the consciousness of the independence of the referent, and thus a very original kind of realism? In Chapter 3, "The Theory of Modern Ontology," of *The Basic Problems of Phenomenology,* Heidegger declares: "For to this very day I am unaware of any infallible decision according to which idealism is false, just as little as I am unaware of one that makes realism true" (p. 167). And on page 170 he states that, "world is only if, and as long as, a Dasein exists." Then he adds, "Nature can also be when Dasein exists."

How can we understand these statements? First *Dasein* in its generality is the quality of Man existing and making possible the being of the world. However, there are existences without Man's presence: this is, I suppose, what Heidegger calls 'Nature.' Then one can see why idealism is not demonstrably false and realism, true. Such a declaration means more than the banal accusation against philosophical incapacity of establishing truth and falsity. The *Dasein* cannot prove that idealism is true, that is, that the world is a construction of the human mind, because the *Dasein* is the experience of the world in its basic independence of the subject; but idealism cannot be proved false, because that independence is understood with-in the understanding of being. On the other hand, realism cannot be proven true, because "independence of the world" is the result of an experience, not its cause.

It seems that Heidegger's statement aims at the traditional distinction between idealism and realism, as it is mentioned in Kant's first *Critique* for instance. Shall we go further and posit that the no-true-no-false situation does apply to Heidegger's philosophy itself? I do not think so. Although it would be futile to start a fight about philosophical labels, I feel that Heidegger's language should be put into the category of *artistic and literary realisms,* as we defined them above, and seen as a kind of *will to reality* opposed to the illusory "belief" of traditional ontologies. Furthermore, the distinction between world and nature seems to imply that Heidegger believed, as many other people do at the level of common knowledge, that there are material, vegetal, animal beings independent of Man's *Dasein* in its thoughts and actions. We could speak of a *concrete, existential realism,* in the same way as literary critics speak of Flaubert's *magic realism,* or as André Breton borrows from Apollinaire the neologism 'surrealism,' thus keeping his distance from the symbolists as well as the realists of the end of the nineteenth century. As such, Heideggerian language makes the *Dasein* an unsurpassable referent. One cannot avoid writing "*Dasein* is . . . and is not . . . ," even if 'is' in this case designates the "praesens" of an understanding.

One may wonder if the great Heideggerian achievement does not lie in the psychology of the referential experience rather than in his own hermeneutics. A very strange psychology indeed! The fascination Heidegger exerted on our minds was due to the invention of a prelinguistic language, a language-of-being before language proper and existences are made possible.

It is immediate perception becoming language before language takes over the control of our thoughts and actions. So, Heidegger made no effort to fight the transparency of language. Far from it. All his efforts were devoted to pulling himself and his readers out of the linguistic world into a pure universe of preconceptual and preverbal experiences, toward a pre-referential referent seen in transparency through the word 'Dasein.' In that perspective, Heidegger is the most authentic *realist of the nonreflective referent*. It means that, in spite of his claim to surpass Kant and to put German language on trial and to test, Heidegger did imply, in the production of his own writing, the two following principles: "language always represents something," and "the something represented is the *cause* of my representation." More directly, *Being and Time* re-presents the *Dasein,* that is, presents the existential experience of the *Dasein* in the form of a system of meaningful signs; or, in more Heideggerian terms, the understanding of Being as perception of things is translated into language: the presentation of Being is then *re*-presented by signs. That implies that the *Dasein* as the being-there is the *cause* of my representation; it produces it. Needless to say, those two concepts of representation and cause intervene in any philosophical realism and, more generally, in any language applied to the languages of perception and action. As a consequence, the true problem concerning representation and causality is not, "What is Representation? What is Causality?" but "*Is 'representation' a necessary word in the language of perception and in the understanding of reference?*" The same question should be considered for 'causality.'

## *The Concepts of Representation and Causality*

There is a de facto answer. Because 'representation' has such a presence and importance in our common, scientific, and philosophical vocabularies, the real problem should not be to know if we can or not dispense with it, but why we cannot avoid it. I disagree with this complacent lexical optimism: the universal use of a term does not demonstrate its necessity; traditions are made of bad habits! Even if for centuries 'representation' was associated with 'language,' we have no right to infer that representation is one of the basic functions of language, or a fortiori that language is the way to express our representation, or that representation is linked to reference (for example, that my reference to that tree implies, at least indirectly, the representation of a "real" tree). To be on safe analytical ground, one must stick to one's methodological nominalist radicalism and raise the following question, *"What is the place of the word 'representation' in a referential system?"* And, first, *What does it refer to?*

A French idealist philosopher, O. Hamelin, published in 1907 a book entitled *Essai sur les éléments principaux de la représentation* (*Essay on the Principal Elements of Representation*). Being an absolute idealist, he explains in the opening of his reconstruction of representational categories that representation represents nothing, but he does not say why the word 'representation' was called upon to designate that operation by which the subject of consciousness constructs its objects and understands them as representation of the world. It would be too easy to observe that a construction is not necessarily a representation, but a referent for potential representation. Then, the realist would exult: the belief in independent reality lurks within the idealist discourse. Here again we find ourselves at the beginning, and positing the existence of an act of perception independent of language . . .

Husserl's phenomenological method helped Maurice Merleau-Ponty to open a subtle path between realism and idealism, empirism and intellectualism: the tree that I perceived as my representation of a tree is not inside my consciousness and not confronted with a real tree; it is the real tree in my backyard. There is no projection of an object by a subject; there is immediate and simultaneous presence of an object perceived and a subject perceiving, understood as exterior/interior within the universal relation of intentionality. In consequence, 'representation,' is a word that refers to a nonlinguistic experience, to what Husserl calls "prereflective Cogito." One may wonder if 'nonlinguistic' and 'prereflective' are quasi-synonymous terms. Thus, the opposition 'exterior/interior,' immanent in the belief in nonlinguistic beings, is closed to the metaphor of the *mirror,* which has pervaded our psychological descriptions since the dawn of Western thought. 'Representation' is used to designate a double reference to an external object in itself and its reflection in a mirror. Merleau-Ponty's

*Phénoménologie de la perception* is revealing: he feels obliged to add a few analyses on language after establishing an autonomous theory of perception, that is a paradoxical nonlinguistic language. More than a language designating nonlinguistic objects, perception is a prelanguage by itself, a representation not yet formulated into language. Doing so, at least in this book, Merleau-Ponty posits the existence of an autonomous field of perception, a prereflective-nonlinguistic field about which he speaks thanks to an organized, reflective language based on the direct distinction between exterior/interior and the image of the mirror. Finally, the mirror plays the role of perception's opposite. Like Hamelin, Merleau-Ponty has to say that representation represents nothing; but how can they explain the simultaneous reference to 'nothing' and/or to nothing?

Can we extract ourselves from those theoretical intricacies? We know (needless to say, 'know' here designates a simple, direct consciousness of meditation entertaining the awareness of its own existence and conditions/implications of existence) that the word 'representation,' in its practical usage, requires the intervention of the opposition 'exterior/interior' and of the mirror metaphor. We know also that it implies the belief in a nonlinguistic state of being—a belief that is the ultimate resource of the realist creed. We know then that such a belief is based on a radical distinction between an external being and an internal being, the second one being the reflection of the other . . . its representation. Consequently, realism is motivated by a belief in the radical duality of 'nonlinguistic/linguistic,' both terms implying the reference to a referent independent of reference. Realism is the brutal invitation to silence intimated by Wittgenstein at the end of his *Tractacus,* preceded by a "It is so and nothing more."

Finally, we should know that there is no clear answer to the idealist provocation: "Representation represents nothing," even if the possibility of a reference to nothing remains a mystery, and thus, that representation cannot, even should not, intervene in the understanding of language. We have to reverse the movement of Merleau-Ponty's first philosophy, and confess that *perception as representation cannot help us to understand language*. For the same reason, the realist belief based on the representation of nonlinguistic beings appears to be a *linguistic postulate;* language, whatever it may be, and language only, can posit the existence of nonlinguistic beings as perceived objects. Heidegger is right: idealism cannot be proved false! To sum up, the concept of representation is of no assistance in the understanding of language. On the contrary, especially in the development of modern philosophy, it has contributed to the obfuscation of the consciousness of language, as if language were a pure and simple signification of our representation and of the represented world. From now on, *I will exclude 'representation' and its innumerable accomplices from our meditation on language*.

Let us make one last effort: if we cannot see how 'representation' is a necessary element in the understanding of language by itself, we could say that 'representation' was introduced among our basic words to refer to a certain experience of the world. But how? it does not matter whether we follow a psychological or a physiological pattern. In both cases, formally, the problem remains the same: I *confer* a certain semanteme on a phoneme in order to be able to *refer* to a supposedly preexisting experience. It means that 'representation' implies a theory—however simple it may be—of representation per se. Thus 'representation,' as meaning, interprets an extralinguistic *X,* which for me becomes 'consciousness' as representation.

There is also another word to designate that *X*—the phoneme 'perception.' Do I state that 'representation' was invented to interpret 'perception' in a metaphorical way thanks to the blessed physical experience of the mirror? It is a sensible hypothesis. As confused as it may be, the history of philosophy, in our modern ages since Descartes and Locke, has turned that metaphor around; any philosophical system was an orchestration of the conceptual vocabulary of Western languages on the theme of representation. It has been a very strange state of affairs: philosophers, busily drawing the maps of the world and of the mind, seemed to have used the word 'representation' as a means of marginalizing the problems of language, even when they were nominalists, and also as a means of building up a translucent castle of concepts worthy of the greatness of Man. Was it not the old dream of *imago Dei* made real by an extraordinary decision of linguistic humility, brilliantly inscribed in Pascal's metaphor of the "thinking reed," or more exactly, of the speaking reed playing at being a "thought," a spiritual light? It is certain that I have not yet answered the question raised at the beginning of the preceding paragraph about the "how" of "representation"; but I understand now that it is a preliminary problem that should uncap the mystifying metaphor of representation. Rephrasing Hamelin's paradox, let us say that *representation does not represent language;* and *language represents nothing, not even itself.* As such, the concept hidden behind the word 'representation' expresses clearly the realist creed of nonlinguistic being but does not justify it; and even less does it justify a realistic interpretation of human knowledge.

Should we take the same attitude before the concept of *causality?* Let us limit ourselves to our present purpose, not considering causality in its epistemological universality. Our problem will be restricted to the case of linguistic causality as hypothetically distinct from physical causality. *Is language the effect of a cause*? It is well known that linguistic sciences at their nineteenth-century beginning decided to ban the problem of the origin of language, which had fascinated grammarians and philosophers of the eighteenth century; to say that language was given to Man by God, or by Life itself, or that it was the product of the collective consciousness of society, is pure and empty transfer or confession of ignorance. Here we face another realist postulate or implication: language, which is part of the physical world, is an aspect of physical causality. But how? The answer is, "Be patient; the physiology of the brain is making its first steps; one day Man will know the cause of his language, even if the word 'cause' takes new and unheard-of meanings." A new invitation to philosophical silence! However, even if a prospective linguistic physicalism is a reasonable hypothesis, it does not mean that a causal problematic of language, in the present state of the semantics of causality, is satisfactory and does not require conceptual revisions, which eventually and indirectly could help specialists of the brain themselves.

Let us consider the two following propositions: "A is the sign of B" and "A is the cause of B." Both are written in a realist mood but initially for two distinct versions of the world—one semiotic, the other physical. Preference for one version or the other can be based on practical reasons; translation of one to the other is possible, as recent theories of communication or cybernetics show; the two semantic fields overlap to the point where the recognition of a sign can be seen as the anticipation of a causal situation, or, in reverse, the designation of a cause invites the vision of a semiotic system. For instance, in the traditional example, the two propositions, "Smoke is the sign of fire" and "Smoke is the effect of fire," differ only in their discursive intention. It is impossible to say that one precedes the other, or that one presupposes the other. Actually, they are simple parts of two parallel languages—a linguistic and a nonlinguistic language. Then we are back to the realist *credo* and its belief in objects independent of language.

In classical epistemology, dominated by a principle of causal irreversibility, physicists could claim that 'causality' was the central scientific concept, when the semiotic relation was an usual part of our common perception. As a result, a scientific theory should be causal, meaning that the perception of a sign should initiate the search for a cause in a physical situation, which is at first received as a scientific state of affairs. However, the more recent concept of structural causality with its synchronic reciprocities, where parts are simultaneously effects and causes, and where there is no precedence between the elements and the totality of a system, suggests that elements and whole coexist in a state of interior determinism, the best model of which is language itself. Then unilinear causal chains in the form of messages emitted and received become integrated parts of a synchronic totality with its diachronic developments. One could imagine a physical semiotics in which language is the sum of independent objects called "objects of the world" in classical physics. Indeed, we know that an epistemology never remains at this stage of vague generalities and that it is accompanied by very complex mathematical analyses and laboratory experiments. But our present meditation on causality does not require reference to such technicalities. It is enough to observe that 'causality' does not help the understanding of 'sign.' Far from it, we could even say that the so-called mysterious power of causality that bothered Descartes, Malebranche, Leibniz, and Hume so much was the projection of the power of the semiotic system of language in an imaginary and convenient world independent of linguistic references.

Nobody has ever answered the *Berkeleyan challenge:* it is impossible to prove that a sensation as psychological atom is the effect of a nonpsychological cause, that is, for instance, that a certain optical vibration, as part of a physical system, is the cause of the red color I just perceived. We are back to Descartes dualist realism, with the juxtaposition of corresponding physical and psychological universes, as opposed to the double possibility of contemporary unifications and reductions—physicalism and psychologism. The only way to answer Berkeley would be to denounce his reverse realistic diktat: the belief in the Divine or human Spirit, as cause of language, is no less arbitrary than the belief in a spatial, independent universe. The causal reasoning, then, takes the following form: language, as known fact, should be explained in reference to an unknown cause we call 'matter' or 'spirit.' Thus, realist philosophy seems to oscillate between a few limited options: distinct or combined physical and spiritual realisms, or, ultimate resource, when one does not dare to maintain the metaphysical belief in material and spiritual substances, agnostic realism without any other presupposition than the existence of reality, whatever it may be.

Before uncapping causality as justification for a realist belief, let us meditate the two following quotations. First André Lalande, in *Vocabulaire technique et critique de la philosophie,*[7] notes that the expression 'transcendental realism' "is used by Hartmann to signify that representation is unseparable from the idea of a cause independent of the will of the subject (*Grundproblem der Erkenntnistheorie,* p. 119);" and Ian Hacking, in a spirit of cheerful irony, quotes Karl Popper:

> I suppose that the most central usage of the term "real" is its use to characterize material things of ordinary size—things which a baby can handle and (preferably) put in his mouth. From this, the usage of the term "real" is extended, first, to bigger things—things which are too big for us to handle, like railways, trains, houses, mountains, the earth and the stars, and also smaller things—things like dust particles or mites. It is further extended, of course, to liquids and then also to air, to gases and to molecules and atoms.
>
> What is the principle behind that extension? It is, I suggest, that the entities which we conjecture to be real should be able to exert a causal effect upon *prima facie* real things; that is, upon material things of an ordinary size: that we can explain changes in the ordinary material world by the causal effects of entities conjectured to be real.[8]

In both quotations 'real' is explained in reference to the psychological experience of human causality and its limitations, that is, its awareness of an "independent cause." For Hartmann it is the experience of the subjective will, reminding us of Maine de Biran's theory of muscular effort or of William James's theory of will as sense of greatest resistance. Popper, in a rather vague manner, imagines the experience of the child and ends with a sort of epistemological principle the origin of which we do not know; to explain changes in the world we must admit the existence of "entities conjectured to be real." Hacking finally approves Popper: "Reality has to do with causation and our notions of reality are formed from our abilities to change the world" (p. 146). For Hartmann as well as for Popper, psychology of will and action helps to understand the learning of the world 'real' and of the belief in a reality independent of language and of the willing of perceiving subject. However, Popper's last phrase warns us that 'real' is a 'conjecture,' not referring to an entity in itself, but conjecturing it. Thus, psychological analysis does not help to make a jump from internal experience to independent referent: a "conjectured identity" is not an entity in itself, but part of language! Psychology can succeed in explaining how in such and such a case, I can 'conjecture' that an entity is 'real' and thus, independent of me, but it cannot understand why independence is used as the criterion of reality, or why causality is the criterion of the independent existence of things and consequently, of reality.

One conclusion only seems to assert itself: neither 'representation' nor 'causality' is of any help in justifying the affirmation of a 'real,' independent referent. Those two terms have muddled the whole of philosophical affairs for more than 2,000 years. It is time to call them off in our attempt to understand and give foundation to our belief in a real world. Is it not strange that no philosopher had ever thought of considering 'real' as referring to an essential part of our linguistic experience, that is, to language as referential and semantic power?

The opposition 'real/unreal' can be interpreted in many ways, such as 'substance/phenomenon,' 'real/imaginary,' 'being/nothingness,' all dualities implying a basic ontological or epistemological system, or a combination of the two in the case of Heidegger's theory of the *Dasein*. "Real," noun or adjective, designates Being or the object of true knowledge; 'unreal' is its negation. How can these oppositions, which look so "natural," be transposed into the linguistic system? If one considers the simple opposition 'language/nonlanguage,' one is led to two paradoxical conclusions: (1) it does not apply, because the opposition to the ontological and epistemological oppositions is that of language of reality contrary to language of unreality, even if they are closely mixed in the production of languages; (2) it amounts to a reverse effect: language is a sort of unreal, when nonlanguage is the real proper. This universal situation, experienced by any user of any language, is often called the *transparency effect,* by Sartre for example, when he uses that visual metaphor to describe the difference between prose (transparent glass) and poetry (frosted or opaque glass). This is not the place to test Sartre's oversimplification; it is a significant expression of literary realism and it shows that 'real,' before designating a nonlinguistic referent as being or object, refers to the most universal condition of language, the so-called transparency: in Saussurian terms, the linguistic sign is more than a relation of a signifier and a signified; it is a signifier conscious of a signified related to a perception (external or internal). In this case, 'to be conscious of' does not describe a psychological state of reflection, but the condition without which language would not be possible. If language were a being with the qualities recognized by traditional or existential ontologies, it would never be language, or it would remain close to certain pathological cases of echolalia. All the same, if language were the result of an epistemological action, that is, a signified arbitrarily completed by a signifier, it would not be language because it would be no more than a series of pointers analogous to highway signals, marking in a very limited way the presence of a collective consciousness in which individual human beings would participate.

In each case, it would be difficult to understand the formation of 'real' as signified and signifier. Let us try to imagine a world (me included) as it would be if the Aristotelian-Thomist ontology were true: each substance in its balance of form and matter has its own becoming made of causes and effects, directed by the power of souls. In such a world, there would be no place for language, except as a mysterious epiphenomenon, a translucent and unnecessary being. After the collapse of the ontological vision, modern thought proposed two models—one physical in the form of a spatio-temporal mechanism, the other spiritual in the form of an autonomous world of representations. In neither of those possibilities does one see where language fits: language is neither an object nor a representation. Reality is well defined as exterior or interior referent; but *realism is only then justified on the basis of the exclusion of language itself:* this philosophical attitude asserts reality in requiring from language a sort of suicide mission.

One understands the raison d'être of the classical ideal: on behalf of truth, reality is conquered thanks to the transparency of language; this is the famous Cartesian clarity qualifying language at the moment of its extreme obliteration. Consequently, realism appears to be not a principle posing the independence of the referent but *a value principle immanent to the production of language,* a value that makes language exist as language of truth, that is, a language that forgets itself in the consciousness of truth. The return from the value principle to the principle of independent referent is all the more understandable as, in its effort to obliterate itself, language has for its main function to forget about itself; by itself it is the genetic *epochè* toward which Husserl was moving but which he finally missed, dazzled as he was by the mirage of intentional transparency.

At this moment of our meditation we can conclude that common and scientific realisms express the basic values of language; they are practical generalizations without which the exercise of language in its relation to action would become an embarrassment. However, they do not justify philosophical realisms in their ontological and epistemological visions. *There is no proof that language presupposes the existence of independent, extralinguistic referents or that the concept of 'extralinguistic being' is just the single and necessary hypothesis that makes language applicable.*

Let us hope that this painstaking and rather boring examination of the implications of the realist belief has been beneficial for our own movement toward a consciousness of language disentangled from a few important conceptual proxies that supposedly contributed to its comprehension. Maybe have we learned something: language does not suffer substitute or cause other than itself, which leads to the following statement in Pascalian style: *Only language speaks correctly about language.* Kant missed his third critical question. In his century as well as ours, the true problem is not: "Is metaphysics possible?," but this double question: "Is ontology possible?" "Is epistemology possible?" To each interrogation the answer should be a clear *No.* Kant's great illusion lies less in his empirical realism than in his transcendental idealism, as a last vain attempt to save the *spiritual proxy* that gave Western cultures their most impressive successes and their flamboyant linguistic cathedrals.

## MEDITATION THREE

# *Uncapping the Psy-Referent and Any Forms of Modern Idealism*

The Kantian model is part of a very general philosophical undertaking that has been at the core of modern speculation. It has been didactically reduced by historians of philosophy to the realist-idealist antinomy. Actually such a problem finds its deep meaning and finality when it is viewed from the referential perspective: whereas realism insists on the independence of the objet of reference as being, idealism underlines the independence of the subject of reference: there is no language without a subject producing discourses and their references. From here, some philosophers pass easily to the conclusion that the object of reference belongs to the subject of reference, that it is not an ob-ject but a pro-ject of the subject. Here one can detect the ambiguity of three centuries of philosophical meditations confusing ontology and epistemology, two so-called basic conditions of language—the ontological one for which there is no language without a being as independent referent, the epistemological one requiring the existence of a subject of thought as cause of language. Thus, depending on philosophical moods, idealism limits itself to a logical problem: Is knowledge possible without consciousness, and is language possible without reference to an independent subject? Or it unveils a secret metaphysical aspiration: Is language possible without the existence of a mind, that is a true metaphysical being? As such, modern idealisms have written variations on the theme of spirituality. Then, the lexicon of mind tends to wrap up and even to replace the lexicon of Being. Was it not the ultimate function of the Cartesian *Cogito*—to affirm that the universal subjective reference of languages implies the existence of a spiritual substance that uses language by accident to express itself in the confused and obscure human condition of the "union of mind and body"? The lexicon of the mind never had the precision of the lexicon of Being, even before sciences imposed the language of mathematics on Aristotelian ontology. In daily usage, almost without noticing it, we pass from 'subject' to 'thought,' to 'mind,' to 'consciousness,' 'unconscious,' 'subconscious,' 'spirit,' 'soul' and their modes, 'understanding,' 'will,' 'reason,' 'imagination,' 'perception,' 'sense,' and so on. Human beings are supposed to deal with these independent referents. To avoid any of the implications and limitations present in each of those terms, I propose to speak of *psy-reference* and its *psy-referents* and to see in idealism a complex modern theory that is trying to explain and justify the *independence of the psy-referents,* whatever vocabulary one may choose. I call 'psy-referent' any kind of hypothetical psychological being—for example, soul, spirit, consciousness, and so on. I call 'psy-reference' the experience by which language affirms the existence of a psy-referent.

The present meditation will be divided into two parts: the first will unfold itself into three moments: (1) a series of critical remarks on the idealist tradition and its contemporary expressions; (2) a reflection on the main justifications proposed for the psy-referent, and (3) an analysis of cultural values that suggests models for the psy-referential world. The second part will be purely critical and will draw conclusions on the millenary belief in the existence of the human mind. The reader who is not versed in philosophical sophistications or who is simply tired of those endless discussions can skip those pages and jump directly to the conclusions, which by themselves will form an autonomous experimental field. Personally, in spite of a strong desire to accelerate this critical movement where I risk being indefinitely bogged down, I feel obliged to review one last time ideas that have controlled my own discourse for about fifty years. Maybe, in the end, I shall be able to use the psy-vocabulary without implying the existence of a referent, be it metaphysical or physiological, without dogmatic arrogance or agnostic refraining.

## *The Psy-Referent and Its Cultural Solicitations*

*The theoretical swamp.* In a book that influenced generations of French philosophy students, *Introduction à la philosophie,*[1] René Le Senne maintains that any philosophical reflection, in its essence and since Plato, is idealist, in the sense that it is a genuine effort to break the realist pattern of common perception and, later, of scientific experimentation. Following Descartes' example, he uses the words 'spirit,', 'thought,' 'mind,' 'consciousness,' as quasi-synonyms. Western philosophy pursued the idealist "conversion" to its ultimate expression in metaphysical spiritualism.[2] Then comes the inevitable conclusion: "Tout est spirituel" [Everything is spiritual]

(p. 250), or in its negative form: "En dehors de l'esprit, il n'y a rien" [Outside spirit there is nothing] (p. 173). Such formulae mean that the distinction between subject and object is immanent to the life of the spirit. Here is the definition of the spirit: "l'unité opératoire d'une relation en exercice, intérieur à lui-même, entre lui-même comme Esprit infini et la multitude des esprits finis" [the operative unity of a relation in action, interior to itself, between itself as infinite Spirit and the multiplicity of finite spirits] (p. 257). The key word of this definition is 'relation' in its double ontological and epistemological dimension: Being = Relation = Spirit, and its double quality of being at the same time one and dual: Spirit = Subject = Subject R Object.

Le Senne's thesis as he conceives it, permits the evaluation of any form of modern idealism as an imperfect approach to absolute idealism. For the moment, it would be useless to get lost into the maze of modern idealisms and their nuances. It is enough to observe that for any form of idealism, the realist belief is seen as an inferior limit of perfection and knowledge, which takes on the meaning of a permanent or relative resistance to the rationalization or idealization of the world. Furthermore, the idealist conversion, which consists in bringing back all existence felt or perceived to aspects of a universal or individual thought, seems unable to avoid the passage to superior referents called Concept, Category, Essence, Value, Transcendantal Subject, or God. When Jules Lachelier remarks: "J'éliminerais l'idée de sujets, distincts de leur représentation, et qui seraient encore à leur manière des choses" [I would eliminate the idea of subjects, distinct from their representation, and which would still be things in their own way],[3] his advice is justified, but is it realizable? What is a subject having no objective reality? There is no possible clear answer to that question because there is no clear definition of the concept of "objective reality." Even if, heeding Lachelier's warning, I declare "not only is the world my representation but I am my representation," I cannot avoid admitting 'I' and 'representation' as referents that are supposedly identical and independent of my language, which can take at least two forms: "I am my representation" and " 'I' is representation." It comes down to saying that I decide to reject the word 'power,' and words like 'cause,' 'source,' and so on. I simply say that I believe in the existence of a subject distinct from objects around me possessing a special way of existing. Thus, idealism inevitably implies spiritualism, the belief in the existence of beings that are not objects—possible, contingent, or necessary—of my perceptions. Lachelier's advice is theoretically attractive but practically untenable.

As a result, there is a sort of connivance between the two philosophical pairs "materialism/spiritualism" and "realism/idealism," that is, an inevitable conspiracy between ontology and epistemology. Modern idealisms after Descartes had hoped to give epistemology a critical independence and to neutralize ontological statements. In fact, they built up a psychological (Hume and his followers) or a logical, moral, or cultural (Kant and his German and French successors) semantics. Thus, any form of idealism separates reference and meaning, rejects reference, and makes of meaning the central question of the philosophy of language. Either reference is recognized and then immediately forgotten in a preliminary theory of sensation (agnostic idealism), or it is assimilated into the dialectical exercise of meaning—one concept referring to another in a sort of permanent and progressive spiral (absolute idealism); but in each case, language in itself is reduced to its exterior, phonetico-grammatical aspects, and doubled by a psychological or dialectical process. Platonic belief in an ideal world pervades the variegated interpretations of the Cartesian *Cogito* and the awareness of the necessary subjectivity of thought.

Le Senne's thesis on the idealist character of any philosophical conversion is correct, once it is completed: Idealism is more than an effort to fight the naturalist objectivism of knowledge and to recognize in the subject (divine or human) the dignity of a free power of eternal or historical creation. It is the will to build up a closed world of meanings and values, an autonomous culture, in brief, a *humanism* capable of absorbing Nature and its species. Eighteenth-century naturalism was a hidden culturalism. Such was the deep sense of Kant's Copernician revolution. Furthermore, as a general grammar, this naturalism was referring language to a state of prelanguage *or* postlanguage, currently called 'mind' or 'consciousness.'

*Is human mind a philosophical myth?* Published at mid-century, *The Concept of Mind* by Gilbert Ryle remains today a constant term of reference.[4] The title suggests that the word 'mind' is a signifier related to a special category of beings themselves called 'concepts.' The naive reader can expect that the book will attempt to explain what sort and what quality of entity is designated by the word 'concept' or, if it is impossible to reach that "natural" goal, what kind of epistemological restriction it implies and what difference there should be between "the concept of mind" and "the word of mind." Ryle's title invites the following (de)finitions or conclusions: "The Physical Being of Mind," "The Spiritual Being of Mind," "The Linguistic Being of Mind," "The Unknowable Being of Mind," and so on. At first view, it is obvious that Ryle, by choosing such a title, hopes to avoid any ontological or epistemological presupposition. He implicitly challenges his readers: "You have to concede me this quasi neutral affirmation: we can only attribute to the word 'mind' in our common and philosophical semantics, the minimal status of a concept. Even to say 'The Word of Mind' would be too committing." Now let us see what Ryle's text is really telling us.

In the opening pages he states that he plans "to rectify the logical geography of the knowledge [about mind] which we already possess" (p. 7). Then, he introduces the Goliath he has to knock out, René Descartes himself, responsible for "a myth which continues to distort the continental geography of the subject" (p. 8). To be more precise, for Ryle, the Cartesian myth is the dualism of mind and matter, or what he calls "the ghost in the machine." Much later Ryle exposes the basic ground of his argumentation and attempts to expel the ghost from the machine: "The general trend of this book will undoubtedly and harmlessly be stigmatised as 'behaviorist' . . . but early behaviorists are in error in accepting a mechanist or para-mechanist theory" (p. 327). Such a statement follows a reflection on the proper status of Ryle's text: it has no scientific pretension; it is an essay on *philosophical psychology*. Then Ryle observes that this necessary recognition draws him onto slippery ground. He attacks the concept of "mental phenomena" as related to "the two-worlds [physical and spiritual] legend" (p. 319). For him " 'psychology' can quite conveniently be used to denote a partly fortuitous federation of inquiries and techniques." The acts of behaviorist faith and hope for a renewed mechanism crowns that interpretation of psychology. Finally, we find out the true purpose of the book: demolishing Cartesian dualism, and thus rendering mind to matter, showing a contrario the truth of the behaviorist theory and replacing a *psychological mythology* by a *philosophical psychology*.

The reader may wonder what Ryle's analysis adds to Locke's or Hume's attempts to go beyond Descartes' dualism and substantialism: it does emphasize the logical dynamism of their psychologist reductions and converts the psy-referent into a physical world with a more refined theory, with a theory that would make psychology independent of physics and biology. Then, Goliath is not defeated: in Ryle's "logical geography," dualism has found another place in the epistemological continent or in the federation of human knowledge (to refer to Ryle's innocent metaphors). However, the last pages of the book volunteer a puzzling remark. On page 329, after reaffirming his general thesis against the Cartesian "two-worlds story," Ryle declares that the Cartesian system is a myth, "though not a fable"; and he hopes that his book has begun "to repair the damage that this myth has for some time been doing inside philosophy." Then, in a rather surprising turn, he pursues: "If, in conclusion we try to compare the theoretical fruitfulness of the Hobbes-Gassendi story of the mind with that of the Cartesians, we must undoubtedly grant that the Cartesian story has been more productive." Indeed, that conclusion is the beginning of another essay on the superior productivity of the Cartesian myth in our modern cultures, with a new question: "Is that productivity exhausted today, or can the Cartesian 'machine' with its ghost be repaired?" Does Ryle mean that behaviorism is the way to repair Cartesian dualism, in integrating it within the patterns of a universal physicalism comprehending a "federation of inquiries and techniques"? Questions without answers, as they are inviting not scientific previsions but pure predictions. Furthermore, they are deeply contradictory: if I knew the future I pretend to foretell, this future would be my present, and I would have no sensible reason for predicting it. The only conclusion we can offer to Ryle's astonishing one, is that we should give up the domain of "philosophical psychology" and try to develop a sort of cultural pragmatics, judging theories from the point of view no longer of their truth but of their more or less durable efficacity. We have heard that theory before! It is even a permanent temptation of the twentieth century's epistemologies. But, if it is rather easy to describe the past efficacity of a theory, how can we determine its future? Ryle, as a philosophical repairman, is not very convincing. To catch him at his own metaphorical game, a repairman repairs, but the progress of knowledge requires the intervention of new machines, be they philosophical or scientific.

We have made no progress in investigating the deep problem of the psy-referent, that is, the formation of a language within language, a language that constitutes a psy-domain. Like Descartes, Ryle does not question the existence of a psy-referent; he just would like to relocate it. Cartesian dualism reappears under a materialist cover, and the act of realist faith in a psy-referent continues to stand in its untouched naivety.

*Naturalization of the psy-referent.* We have already mentioned the profession of naturalism in John Searle's philosophy of language, well known for his theory of speech acts, which was a first attempt to interpret language within the frame of a natural psy-referent. Recently he completed his transposition in making of language behavior an aspect of a more general quality, specific to living beings. He calls it the *intentionality of the mind.* See in particular *Intentionality, an Essay in the Philosophy of the Mind*

(1983), *Mind, Brain, and Science* (1984). In the former, Searle's basic geography opens with an initial statement as clear as possible: "Philosophy of language is a branch of the philosophy of the mind" (p. vii). He specifies: "The capacity [for sentences] to represent is not intrinsic but derived from the Intentionality of mind." Other qualifications are added: "The forms of Intentionality underlying language are social forms . . . people have mental states which are intrinsically Intentional" (p. viii). Rejecting behaviorism and functionalism, he promotes a biology of "mental phenomena." Finally, probably to take his distance from the great thinkers of intentionality, in a rather arrogant way, he declares that "he decides to ignore the philosophical past of Intentionality" (p. ix). After all, it is his right to do so and to discard lightly one of the most important enterprises in rejuvenating philosophical language in the nineteenth and twentieth centuries. In any case, in the first pages of *Intentionality,* Searle posits an array of prerequisite synonyms in order to ascertain the objective status of the psy-referent:

Psy-referent = Mind = Brain = Biological capacities to relate organisms to the world = Mental states = Intentionality = Social Forms.

Let us add an inequality that qualifies this rather hazy continent: Intentionality ≠ Computability.

Searle's *Intentionality* is a sort of disguised treatise on human nature that transposes the Humean psy-problematic into the language of biological logic: problems of perception, meaning, and causation are successively discussed. One only regrets that Searle stops short of facing the traditional problem of the subject and the self. One wonders if a theory of intentionality can be complete without an analysis of the concept of subjectivity: for instance, what do belief, desire, fear, and the like mean for modes of existence such as representation, causation, consciousness? Even if one should conclude that subjectivity is illusory, that the self does not exist in itself any more than free will is possible (see Searle's final Reith Lecture), it is impossible to bypass the problem of biological individuality. If intentionality is formalized as $xRy$ (and we suppose, at least out of temporary convenience, that $R$ is identical to $I$ for intentionality), $x$ and $y$ are not undifferentiated quantities: $x$ is the subject of intentionality; $y$, its object. Their duality is irreducible. Without going as far as Cartesian substantialist dualism, we must explain the difference between $x$ and $y$, even at the lowest level of biological description. The lesson of the *Cogito* cannot be discarded. It is too easy and vague to write "fundamental capacities of the mind (or brain)." For both the mind and/or the brain, there is no such reality as the mind in general, the brain in general. The real thing is my brain, your brain,

Searle's brain writing his books, and so on. Even if the brains of the individuals in a given species were identical, that identity would not eliminate the problem of individuation of such and such animal and especially the problem of the individuation of the brain.

The absence of a theory of the self and of individuation does not mean that Searle is wrong in making of intentionality the universal property of the psy-referent integrated to the more general bioreferent under the protection of scientific research. My present purpose is to understand how Searle handles the problem of the independence of the psy-referent. His anti-idealist position is clear: intentionality is not to be confused with consciousness; these two classes of concept overlap, but there is no possible inclusion of one in the other. (See his Chapter 1: "The Nature of Intentional States.") In the same way, his realism is biologically rooted. Let us take another look at a text already discussed: "*Realism,* I want to say, is not a hypothesis, belief, or philosophical thesis; Realism is part of the Background in the following sense: My commitment to "realism" is exhibited by the fact that I live the way I do, I drive my car, drink my beer, write my articles, give my lectures, and ski my mountains" (pp. 158–59). He adds the following declaration: "Contemporary discourses of realism are, for the most part, strictly senseless, because the very posing of the question, or indeed of any question at all, presupposes the preintellectual realism of the Background. . . . [Realism] is not a hypothesis at all, but the precondition of having hypotheses" (p. 159). In other words, realism is *the* precondition of language. Obviously it is a perfect circle, plus a sort of "linguistic argument," shaped on the medieval or Cartesian ontological proof of the existence of God, as exhibited and condemned by Kant: the essence of language should imply the existence of a reference for the same reason that the essence of God implies his existence. Consequently, in a paradoxical way, realism, common or philosophical, presupposes the absolute idealism of the ontological proof. Furthermore, the main argument concerning the existence of language as necessarily referred to the existence of an independent referent, as well as its theological translation, offers a deceptive evidence: there is no dawn of a logical or experimental proof in the affirmation of the necessity of an independent referent, explaining the existence of language. I do not see why language could not exist in itself, and its referents be effects of its references. At least it is a perspective worth exploring. In spite of Searle's conclusion, an idealist driver is conceivable: one can be idealist in interpreting the environment as a system of pure signifiers and driving through it while avoiding accidents! After all, a drunken driver is not necessarily idealist; he can be a realist who miscalculates the place and resistance of the referents he perceives—a realist who, like Searle, decides to ignore the idealist implication of his pragmatic belief.

Considering the present imbroglio, one will not be suprised to observe Searle reducing his array of synonyms into a basic one: Intentionality = Meaning, then proposing a theory of proper names that is nothing more than a corollary of his realist act of faith. In the central chapter of his book, "Are Meanings in the Head?," he attacks Putnam's realism as expressed in "Meanings are not in the Head."[5] Searle extends Frege's concept of "*Sinn*" to that of intentionality and makes a linguistic reference a "special case of Intentional Reference" (p. 197).

The affirmation of an external referent is subordinated to the belief in an internal referent—the human brain. Searle calls himself an *internalist* (see p. 198) in the sense that it is in virtue of some mental state in the head of a speaker and hearer that one can understand linguistic references. Internalism is the philosophical option according to which "the brain is all we have in the purpose of representing the world to ourselves and everything we can use must be inside the brain." Searle explains his rallying to Frege on behalf of "a kind of biological phenomenon and it is part of the natural world like any other phenomenon" (p. 230).

Plato and Kant especially are not far away! Do we have to call Searle's internalism and biologization of the concept of intentionality a kind of idealism? Indeed, it would be unfair to treat Searle like a disguised immaterialist or spiritualist. However, it is obvious that he falls back into a modern revision of Descartes dualism: behind the biological cover-up, the space/mind duality is restored under the distinction made between the exterior world and the internal brain. Consequently for Searle, the natural belief in an external world depends upon the reality of the brain and on its power of representation. This boils down to saying that language implies an internal referent in order to explain the external one. *Is this not pure idealism in a biological fashion?*

Our basic objection reappears in a new form: if the belief in an external referent is justified by the parallel existence of an internal referent called the brain, what is the justification for this internal referent? Is language impossible without the hypothesis of the existence of the brain/mind? This time, Searle can no longer invoke the common sense of the driver. He simply speaks in the name of scientific realism, *but* in a domain that is beyond the limits of neuropsychology. Once more, let us insist on the fact that a proposition such as "intentionality is a biological phenomenon"

(p. 230) is *not* a scientific description but an undercover philosophical generalization. It also demonstrates that internalism and the restoration of a neoCartesian dualism within a physicalist pseudo-unity are inherent parts of modern cultural semantics; but they do not prove that they cannot offer a theory of language without their help. They just show that the reference to an internal power of linguistic representation leads to a philosophy that, beyond physicalism or naturalism, reorganizes itself as *cultural relativism,* that is to say, as a new conception of the psy-referent that hopes to surpass the deadlock of any form of realism as well as the spiritualist conversion of modern idealism.

*The case of Nelson Goodman.* In his book *Of Mind and Other Matters* (1984), which intends to reconsider the dominant topics discussed in *Languages of Art* (1968) and *Ways of Worldmaking* (1978), Nelson Goodman assigns himself a place within the philosophical world and takes his distance from some of the *-isms* that serve as milestones in our modern epistemological reflective labyrinth. Already in *Ways of Worldmaking* he had dated the beginning of his critical reflection from the time when Kant exchanged the structure of the world for the structure of the mind. In our present meditation it would mean that Goodman sees in Kant the philosopher who transferred the traditional reference to an external reality called 'world' to an internal reality called 'mind.' However, when one lives and thinks in the second part of the twentieth century, one can no longer believe in the reality of the universal structure of human reason and thus, the possibility of a universal truth. Goodman is a pluralist of sorts: Man's cultures are made of visions or versions of world. Enlightenment relativism has been blown up into a *pluralistic culturalism,* a diversity of "styles of representation and understanding," expressing multiple processes of physical and artistic worldmakings. Indeed, Goodman feels the need for a new philosophical specification, and in the Preface of *Of Minds and Other Matters* he defines the uniqueness of his general position as follows:

> I am a relativist who nevertheless maintains that there is a distinction between right and wrong theories, interpretations, and works of art . . . ; I am a nominalist who lets anything be taken as an individual, and a rather behavioristically oriented cognitivist who recognizes the cognitive function of emotion. I am an anti-realist and an anti-idealist—hence an irrealist. I oppose both the scientism and humanism that set the sciences and the arts in opposition to each other. And I am a theorist concerned with practice as informing and informed by theory.[6]

Among the *-isms* mentioned in this neat summing up, the key word is *irrealist,* which is later analyzed (p. 29 and ff.): it does not mean that everything is irreal but that the world melts into versions making worlds; and there are discussions about the rightness of versions of a well-built world. It is revealing that Goodman never offers a direct theory of the mind. Surely there are in his writings substitutes like 'thought,' 'understanding,' and also an implied synonym: mind refers to "art in act," as if, coming back to Kant's three *Critiques,* Goodman were integrating the first two theoretical and practical reasons into the aesthetic judgment, that is, into a certain and unspecified activity of the human mind understood as a given culture and/or a given person.[7] Goodman's last statement concerning an implied verificationism or experimentalism (the well-known shuttle between ideas and facts) makes us wonder if he really succeeds in going out of the Kantian epistemological polarization between transcendental idealism and empirical realism, and thus, between the two unknown aspects of the thing in itself—the mind and the world. Cartesian dualism then reappears at the level of a confessed agnosticism!

Furthermore, in spite of Goodman's protests, there is still another dualism that is not overcome—that of the arts and the sciences. Let us accept Goodman's theory according to which there are different symbolic systems functioning in the creation and understanding of our worlds, and, consequently, that scientific and artistic productions belong to the universal category of symbolizations.[8] It will remain to be explained why and how sciences and arts have historically diverged in our Western cultures. Historical relativism does not go further than pure observation. When, at the conclusion of *Of Mind* Goodman notes that, "in our culture arts are not really taken seriously" (p. 150), to what category of knowledge does such a statement belong? It seems to be part of a cultural analysis or sociology of culture. Should we call it scientific? More generally, to what system of discourse does Goodman's defense of the arts belong? When in *Languages of Art* he states that aesthetic experience is a reorganization of the world in terms of works and of works in terms of worlds, and as such, is a form of understanding, his writing can be classified as aesthetic criticism.[9] Today discussions continue to be wide open on the scientific or philosophical status of that language. To use Goodman's terms, it belongs to the referential mode of denotation, not to that of exemplification. To what else does philosophy belong? Goodman cannot avoid "working" his own language within an array of dualities: science/art, science/philosophy, denotation/exemplification, world/mind. If I follow correctly his reasoning, human mind is the power of worldmaking. But it seems that Goodman refuses to make the idealist leap and to absorb exteriority into the interior worlds of the creative mind. If this is so, he is a hidden phenomenologist: the Husserlian couple *noema/noesis* is interpreted as the interrelation "world/work."

In this case, as in the parallel case of Ryle, Searle, and many others, Cartesian dualism is surreptitiously reestablished, as if any form of reductionism, that is, any effort to build up a unique frame of reference, took on the aspect of a bidimensional universe with the axis of the world and the axis of the mind, or, in other words, a double—objective/subjective—system of reference, which is itself anchored in the two independent referents of the world and the mind. To say that they are inseparable does not alleviate the mystery of their existence.

At this moment, restricting myself to the only consideration of the psy-referent, should I say that all those philosophical intricacies and involuntary implications lead to the necessary conclusion that I cannot speak or write without accepting, consciously or not, the existential postulate of the mind? The behaviors of the three philosophers we have just observed betray, in their own language and style, a very singular situation: they reject all the traditional philosophical justifications of the psy-referent, but they reintroduce it in various disguises. Descartes is their scapegoat. However, to replace the word 'God' by the words 'Nature' or 'Culture' does not authorize the ontological Cartesian coup de force and does not remove our language from idealist implications. Is it not naive to pile up book after book just to conclude: Let the scientist (whatever he may be, whatever his methods are) do his job? Once more, why not follow the advice Wittgenstein did not apply to himself: Stay silent!

Maybe our great predecessors were not as stupid as our arrogance makes them out to be. Maybe we should also take a new look at Noam Chomsky's Cartesianism and see how the concept of mind has succeeded in cohabiting with his system of universal grammar?

*The search for a new mentalism, or another avatar of the psy-referent.* Let us investigate the basic notions of generative grammar as parts of an interpretation of the psy-referent, building up linguistics on the independence of a *reality* named 'mind' and fighting for an internalist realism. The semantic status of Chomsky's texts is not easy to determine. For instance, one of his books, a sort of summing up of his theory, is entitled *Language and Mind* (1972) and is divided into three parts analyzing the past, the present, and the future of "Linguistic contributions to the study of Mind." Linguistics is classified as part of human psychology and more specifically, of cognitive psychology.[10] In the Preface Chomsky forcefully exposes his deep convictions: "I believe and try to show in these essays, that the study of language structures reveals *properties of mind* that underlie the exercise of *human mental capacities* in normal activities, such as the use of language in the ordinarily *free and creative fashion*" (p. vii; my italics). After years of reflection on Chomsky's philosophical implications (I am not a linguist and do not pass judgment on the importance of his contributions to linguistics), I arrive at the following conclusion: his "study of Mind" is inspired by three convictions that are interrelated but in a nonsystematic way. I will call them the *methodological*, the *epistemological*, and the *ontological* decisions.

The first one answers the question, "How does one make a science of language that will not be superficial and trivial?" There is only one way: "to move beyond superficiality by a readiness to undertake perhaps far-reaching idealization and to construct abstract models that are accorded more significance than the ordinary world of sensations."[11] One understands why, in that perspective, behaviorism as well as Piaget's genetic psychology are accused by Chomsky of being trivial, that is, unable to be proved true or false: any attempt at the reconstitution of psychological processes (language included) implies an *abstract model* that can be tested by well-chosen examples. It also points to the polemical aspect of Chomsky's innatism and his call for Descartes' patronage: his is not a psychological but a *methodological innatism.* It is clear that Chomsky's methodological principle is idealist in spirit although it does not imply the Schopenhauerian belief that "the world is my representation." It only means that to represent reality, especially psychological reality, I must imagine abstract representations, not mental states but mental models. The behaviorist and genetic schemes are purely descriptive and explain nothing.

At this point the philosopher could withdraw, refuse to enter the battlefield, and invoke a criterion of historical efficiency: perhaps the future will tell us who among you, social or human scientists, is successful. In the meanwhile, I cannot help noticing that Chomsky does not succeed in keeping up a strict methodological attitude. His adversaries draw him willy-nilly into the domain of epistemology and the intricacies of the relation of physics and psychology. First Chomsky seems to fall into the methodological circle in a very Cartesian way. After saying that to explain human mind one must imagine "abstract models," he notes: "It may be true that the mind is so constituted that it constructs regular geometrical figures as 'exemplars' for the interpretation of experience" (p. 38). Is it not a sort of physicalism and naturalism, human mind with its properties being part of nature? Thus, the term 'mind' is a substitute for the term 'brain,' or at least it designates some properties of the brain. Finding the difference among Chomsky, Putnam, Searle, and others, one would rely on a manner of interpreting physicalism, in particular the relation of psychology and neurobiology. Chomsky takes two apparently contradictory stands: on the one hand, although a physical explanation is possible, it is far remote: "It seems futile to speculate about matters so remote from present understanding." (*Language,* p. 98); on the other hand, "these [biological] properties determine the kinds of cognitive systems, language among them, that can develop 'universal grammar' to refer to the properties of human biological endowment" (*Rules,* p. 28). The confrontation of those two statements suggests some epistemological options. First a practical one: in the present state of its methods and theories neurobiology is unable to offer an explanation of mind, and there is no reason to stay inactive and to wait for the moment it is ready. Linguistics, Chomsky style, would be a sort of "waiting for the biological Godot." Second, the present theory of "cognitive systems, language among them," with its construction of abstract models, is already an explanation of the "human biological endowment," even without reference to the cerebral system. Then, we come into a very complex epistemological state of affairs: those abstract models (why not call them 'abstract machines'?) are more than temporary explanations; they show how the human mind works; they even permit building up concrete machines analogous to the human mind. The old dream of seventeenth-century mechanism finds a new means of expression.

The present debate around computer models is the best proof that Chomsky's epistemological principle is far from being clear; it contains many implications that leave open the traditional philosophical problem, "Is mind different from nature?" Even if mind is part of nature, is that part distinct from the other parts? Is the brain an organ analogous to the heart or the liver? Physicalism recuperates the old categorical opposition between unity, duality, and plurality. In the present state of biological theories, there is no reason to favor one term or the other of those three possible systematizations. It seems that Chomsky opposes the behaviorist reductionism and prefers a kind of dualism based upon a Leibnizian "*Nihil est in intellectu quod not prior fuerit in sensu, nisi ipse intellectus*" [There is nothing in the mind that is not to be found first in the senses, except for the mind itself]. Linguistic performance and its environment imply an innate structure that is independent of external actions upon it. That belief asserts the epistemological autonomy of the psy-referent and consequently, of psychology itself, the only reservation being the future, remote, and unpredictable reference to neurobiology's developments. This time, Chomsky cannot invoke the possibility of experimental verification, as he did for his methodological principle. I am afraid that his epistemology, no different from any other, does not go beyond the trivialities he happily denounced in Piaget or Skinner. Here we are dealing with basic decisions that reveal a very strange situation: the idealism of the methodological principle is in a way compensated for by the realism of the epistemological one, the right of building up abstract models is justified by this condition: there are unknown psy-systems with which the abstract models can be confronted.

It is obvious that this epistemological realism hides a mysterious *ontological principle,* without which we could not explain the constant use of the term 'mind.' We can give it the following formulation: "There is a reality, which is called 'mind,' and is *cause* of human psychological conducts, language among them." Indeed Chomsky does not fall into the Cartesian spiritualist substantialism: "I am a finite thinking substance created by the infinite thinking substance." But he is not far from it. 'Mind' is never specifically defined. Its meaning is implied through expressions such as "mysterious ability of language creativity," "language as instrument of free thought and expression" (*Language,* pp. 100 and 102). In *Rules,* from the outset he declares: "When I use such terms as 'mind,' 'mental representation,' 'mental computation,' and the like, I am keeping to the level of abstract characterization of the properties of certain physical mechanisms, as yet *almost entirely unknown.* There is no further *ontological import* to such reference to mind or mental representation and acts" (p. 5; my italics). This quotation clearly proves that Chomsky is conscious that his epistemology is navigating close to the medieval ontology of obscure forces called 'faculty,' 'capacity,' or 'property.' However, with a clean conscience, he does not hesitate to speak of "human language faculty" (pp. 25 and 45), "faculties of the mind" (p. 28), "number faculty," "cognitive faculties," "rich innate endowment" (p. 45), although he says that there is no "ontological import" in those phrases. Is it so sure? Is there not a contradiction in speaking of "physical mechanisms" that are "unknown"? If this is the case, what does 'physical' mean? Furthermore, what is the "ontological import" of "abstract characterization" of linguistic properties? Even within the limit of an epistemological agnosticism that could be referred to Kant, those abstractions must have something to do with the faculties they refer to. Thus, if we follow correctly Chomsky, we must conclude that there is an unknown physical reality we call 'human mind' that is the mysterious cause of diverse psychological abilities—the ability to feel, the ability to know, the ability to create and learn languages, and "our ability to choose and decide what we will do" (*Rules,* p. 46) Are we not back to the endemic and nagging problem of traditional or modern psychology? How many faculties? Can they be reduced to three, to two, to one? What are the relations of perception to language and thought? Finally, this great theoretician of language uses the word 'mind' to give to language a referent independent of all its other referents. Instead of saying in Descartes' company "my mind is substantially different from my body," he presupposes (since there is no scientific proof and he is using trivial language) that human mind, cause of language, is at the same time part of and distinct from my body. Biology knows a little about the body, almost nothing about the mind, although one thing is certain: our present conception of physical beings does not apply to our mind, even if we are sure that our mind is physical.

What can a philosopher do who claims neither to complete the knowledge of physics and biology, nor to propose a definition of the properties that characterize physical beings? He cannot give up his meditative experience and decide on a radical, silent skepticism because he feels that there is something more to experience through the transparency of the referent than to insist on the autonomy and independence of the psy-referent. In other words, let us face the question directly: *"Why do we normally believe in the existence of a being called 'mind' that is cause of language?"*

## *Processing the Psy-Referent, or the Great Self-Abnegation of Language*

The above discussions lead to the conclusion that, far from being incompatible epistemological theories, realism and idealism are complementary systems aiming at the explanation of language on the basis of two referents, one external, the other internal, one being the object of language, the other its subject. Posing these two principles in the necessary form of existential judgments, neither epistemology can avoid a sort of double ontological implication: language implies the existence of double ontological implication: language implies the existence of beings as objects and subjects. Then philosophies of language give a new interpretation to the old opposition between materialism and spiritualism, even when they do not mention those terms and when they hide their conceptual confusion behind the term 'naturalism.' Furthermore, idealism is in the same lexical situation as 'realism': its existential judgment concerning the subject of language is pure postulation. There is no proof—either deductive or inductive, either positive or negative—of the existence of a subject as source, production, and medium of language. This is as if language by itself was looking for its existence and essence outside itself and, especially, imagining a world of which the language world would be a part. Let us formulate the paradox of that strange intellectual muddle: to ascertain its own existence and understanding, language seems to be forced to require the existence of a psy-model-and-world inaccessible in itself, only indirectly tested through language. Language is unable to go out of itself. As Hegel justly said, "the perfect element within which interiority is as exterior as exteriority is interior, is language."[12] In other words, when language refers to something other than itself, it is still linguistic decision and operation. It is as if to be language, language has to negate itself and believe in the existence of a human mind. It is in the "nature" of language to fight against its own linguistic condition. Linguistic expression is the permanent process of the fight of language against itself: *to be language I have to forget that I am language.*

Why? The question has a psycho-linguistic import. We are leaving the epistemological domain and its problem with no exit. We are also leaving Kant's critical philosophy, which, in our century, has remained the secret and seldom unrecognized refuge of many ungrateful philosophers. I mean that I can no longer feign to explore a linguistic conceived a priori as a system of universal and necessary conditions without which humanity and its cultures would be impossible, and to write for our era a new *Critique of Linguistic Reason.* Looking at our philosophical past, I can merely seek other arguments than those extolled by realist and idealist epistemologies.

The most tempting solution would be a psychoanalytical interpretation of language fighting itself and denying to itself the status of a real being. I could also read Lacan on the "discourse of the Other," meditating on the experience of Otherness as language producer and receiver. In another direction I could see in language a double conduct of frustration and sublimation in the spirit of Freud's theory of Art and the artist: Human mind would be a mythopoetic imaginary that is invented by our language power to escape the unpleasantness of linguistic realities into a place of transparent visions and free pleasure. Man, ill at ease in his linguistic natural condition, would build up a fictive universe of psychological relations and, in a convenient slip, forget that this universe by itself is made of words. In a word, reference to mind would lose itself in complacent phantasms. The psychoanalytic cure would consist of a transfer from a pathological language to a language accepted as the true interpretation of preinfancy and infancy events projected into conscious life. In that case, psychoanalysis would be reintegrated in the field of psycho-linguistics. Consequently, the individual pathological behavior would be a particular manifestation of the general pathology of psy-referential life thanks to the hypothetical theater of an independent referent called 'mind.' The free association language, like psychoanalytical therapy, would serve as a slow and difficult transition between the first and wrong systematization to the final and right one, that is, between the linguistic escape from language to the return to the peace of language accepting itself without the help of the mind and its mythical referents.

Freud's implicit materialism and naturalism are then understood at their deepest level: psychoanalysis would be a therapeutics tending to restore language to its original vocation. Finally, languages of mind, in their diversity and complexity, would be the effects of historical misuses of the brain. Here again we meet the brain model and neurophysiology with its remote expectations. We can also detect another implication latent in Ryle, Searle, and other naturalists and, more generally, since the naturalism of the Enlightenment: Why are things going wrong in their natural processes? What is the meaning of right and wrong, pathological and normal, in such situations? In the case of the mind referent, why does language need the illusions of an escape from itself, and why is man dreaming of transparent castles, which after all are nothing more than linguistic organizations centered around the word 'mind' or its convenient synonyms?

To sum up, psychoanalysis is a very dramatic attempt to reconstruct the autobiographical languages that accompany all human lives from birth to death and to rectify their referential consciousness. The problem of its usefulness is purely pragmatic; it does not belong to the field of philosophical meditation. However, psychoanalysis, especially when it becomes an interpretation of the deep reasons why language fights itself, deserves the attention and the respect of the philosopher. It can help to elucidate that *pessimism* present at the heart of linguistic usages and is related to a *transparency complex* at the source of any form of idealism or realism.

*The Locke effect.* There is still another argument that is omnipresent in any theory of language after Descartes, that is behind modern linguistics's pessimism and the dream of linguistic reform. I propose to call it the *Locke effect* because Locke was one of the first to associate epistemology and theory of language, simultaneously opening the way to eighteenth-century psychologism and analytism. In its simplest form, the Locke effect states that *there are more meanings than words*. There is an essential impotence in language: I cannot express what I feel and think; my language is always inadequate in quality and quantity; there is always more to say, and it should be told differently! Furthermore, by nature, as social instrument of communication, language is abbreviative. It looks for the easiest and shortest way to transport and transfer ideas: Locke condemns rhetoric and compares it to the fair sex and its artificial devices.

Linguistic life is torn out between two contradictory experiences and their opposite values—that of meaning and that of communication. Signs stand for ideas, but there are many more ideas than signs, and it would be impossible to invent signs for all ideas (sensations and images) that happen in our minds. The infinite field of psychology surrounds the restricted field of linguistic signs, like the Ocean's waves along the beaches of an island. On the other hand, communication requires abbreviation and simplicity, when meaning invites more refinement and complexity. Language is at the same time a poor translator and transporter of the activities of our minds but a very efficient tool for social relations. Neither our speech nor, even less, our writing, can compete with the internal complexity and speed of our psychological exchanges, but they are the necessary and practical devices that maintain human societies in existence and movement.

For the moment I reserve the elusive problem of the meaning of meaning, and of the meaning of the experience present behind the Locke effect. Our meditation will only be devoted to the processes leading to the vision of a psy-referent inaccessible to sign ingenuity.

Berkeley drew the radical conclusion from the Locke effect: if the realm of ideas challenges its reduction to signs, if languages are absolute forgeries, then why not put aside language and live within the world of ideas? Berkeley's abolition of language is solicited by the metaphor of "drawing the curtain": "We need only to draw the curtain of words to behold the fairest tree of knowledge." Let us appreciate the optimism suggested by the adverb 'only,' a true continuation of the Cartesian *Cogito* and its consequence: "Mind is easier to know than body." Linguistic transparency is there at its best! When Berkeley writes his invitation to draw the curtain of words, he does not see the words he is writing; he confers upon the chosen metaphor the ontological power of passing from one world to another. More specifically, he passes from the world of language to the world of vision and transparency. The image of the window is both a poetic and pictorial one. It has fascinated poets and novelists as well as painters. It is frequently associated with the image of interior and closed rooms, prisons and, with their opposites, open, empty spaces, large horizons. It suggests the infinite of another world opposed to the finite of the room. Before Berkeley, Descartes again, in the Third Meditation, imagined himself at a window looking at the passersby. Furthermore, windows are also images for the eyes: instruments of vision, turned toward the exterior reality, and also mirrors of the soul, eyes getting access to the two universes of mind and body. So the metaphor of the window eye invites its annulment between two opposed images, what Berkeley, with many others, calls the perceived and the perceiving. The Cartesian unity of mind and body is thus reduced to the linguistic operation, the only word opacity between the double and immaterial transparency of the beings perceived and perceiving.

Such is the great Berkeleyan lesson: the duality of mind and body, which Descartes in his "problematic idealism" (to borrow Kant's expression) had clearly put out of the empirical world, is actually the direct consequence of our linguistic condition. The meditating Descartes never succeeds in forgetting that, by a mysterious and divine decree, Man is a dual reality made of spiritual and material essences. He remains a realist in spite of his meditations. His doubt is not as radical as he thinks. Going further Berkeley radicalizes the experience of the *Cogito* by the double metaphorization of the window and the curtain as double powers of transparency and opacity. He proceeds to a hyperphenomenal suspension that Husserl never consciously attempted—*the existential suspension of language by itself.* The window is the image of the escape from the language world, the image of the liberation of Man from the linguistic condition. Berkeley's "immaterialism" really means "surnominalism," access to the surreality of images beyond the screens of words.

The Locke effect takes its full existential value within the Berkeleyan abolition of language: curtain drawn, an infinite universe of spiritual qualities is displayed in front of me as I approach the state of pure vision surpassing opacity; the immense ocean of images and meanings plays the eternal game of divine creation. The window and its drawn curtain take on a double value: when I draw the "curtain of words" I reach a state of spiritual transparency, beyond the illusory domain of physical transparency. In a way, the curtain of words is like a stage curtain portraying physical reality. Drawing it, it is as if I were also drawing a veil over the external universe, closing the curtain, not opening it. In the room of the

*Cogito,* all curtains closed, a new world of ideas appears, richer and "fairer" than the realm of words.

Hume completed Berkeley's radicalization of the *Cogito.* He converted immaterialism into phenomenism, liberating himself from the spiritualist referent. Freed from language and from any kind of referents, images float in a sort of psychological sea, regulated by the laws of association. The Locke effect, through Berkeley and Hume, gave to modern thought its basic implications: on one hand, it leads to Kant's criticism and to the construction of an a priori system of concepts founding scientific laws; on the other, it opens the way to three centuries of more or less successful researches called "human sciences." However, in itself, the Locke effect continued to be taken for granted: it stayed unexplored, unexplained, like the *Cogito* and its supposed clarity. Here is the problem we should face now, but while staying inside our linguistic experience: *what is the raison d'être of the Locke effect if we consider that its implications concerning the existence of a dual universe of words and ideas are not acceptable?*

A first try would consist of seeing in this effect a universal linguistic experience and of applying it to the brain model. Linguistic operations, we suppose, are preceded by a great number of physiological impressions; thanks to still unknown processes these impressions are stored in our brains; then the symbolic mechanisms of language intervene to concentrate the dust of perceptions so that the so-called representations of the brain are projected into a world of words, which is to the world of cerebral representation in the same relation as a rough draft is to a realistic drawing. As already noted, the brain model does not help to clarify a linguistic experience. It is just an invitation to wait. It relies too much on unknown expectations, and it raises questions more than it offers a theory, except at the very vague level where today's naturalisms take refuge. Furthermore, it does not show what kind of experience is just translated into the dualism of ideas and words. Even if I imagine, within the brain, the opposition between the quasi-infinite world of impressions and the finite world of linguistic signs, I do not explain why the preliminary impressions are understood as meanings preceding the actual exercise of language. I do not avoid the paradox we already faced of a language positing the existence of a prelanguage of meanings and even of a language of independent objects (the well-known object-language of the logicians). To sum up, the brain model, in the present state of neuropsychology, is a physiological translation parallel to the psychological one imagined in the post-Cartesian era. The philosophical implications of the brain model are analogous to those of the psy-referent.

Once more we are brought back to our rule of linguistic restriction and wisdom: with a linguistic problem look for a linguistic solution. When the time comes, if it comes, and only then, our present rule will become obsolete. In the meanwhile we should think that only language can legitimately speak about language and find in itself the understanding of its processes and experiences. Let us reformulate our present question: *How can it happen that I become conscious of a discrepancy between what I feel and what I say?* Thus expressed my question has a dangerous psychological flavor. It could invite us to the seduction of an analysis, Humean type. Maybe, but with one important difference: I do not imply the existence of a psy-referent; I just posit the existence of a consciousness of language by itself; the feeling I refer to is of psycho-linguistic order; I do not suggest that we should come back to introspection or to a behaviorist description; I simply try to understand in what conditions language speaking about itself turns into a language against itself and becomes conscious of the limits of its semantic power. May I even confess that, not believing in the psychological existence of a human consciousness, I think that by itself consciousness is a strictly linguistic operation.

Let us examine a few examples of statements (not hypothetical psychological states of affairs) implying the duality idea/word. "John stays silent. However, he thinks a lot," his mother says. A rather common observation that comes from the distinction between thinking and speaking, between interior and exterior languages and that leads to the remark that the language expressed through voice or other means is just the tip of everybody's linguistic iceberg. From there one goes to the collateral observation: "We can never express all we think or feel. We could say more than we actually say." Reasons for that situation are diverse: We do not have enough time, we prefer not to express all our thoughts, we even prefer to lie. In those cases, the duality idea/word does not denounce a linguistic failure. On the contrary, a specific power of language is acknowledged: the communication of thought is controllable. I can choose to say more or less than I am really thinking; and 'thinking' means potential or interior speeches, that is, references to the consciousness of linguistic virtualities. My thought is not grammatically and semantically shaped; but I know that, if necessary, I could do the proper encoding, although my semantic confidence can appear to be illusory or too optimistic.

*La parole intérieure.* It would be tempting to invoke the Chomskyan duality of competence and performance, but it would not strictly coincide with the duality thought/language or its synonyms. The consciousness of my competence (let us say in French as in English) is not identical with my consciousness of possible and unexpressed performances. The Chomskyan duality concerns a faculty and its manifestations. On the other hand, the duality thought/language deals with performance only and is based upon the duality that seems to be characteristic of the performance experience: there are expressed and unexpressed performances. Psycho-linguistics has always been interested in that phenomenon. One may remember *La Parole intérieure* by Victor Egger (1881). More recently L. S. Vygotsky's study *Thought and Language*[13] explores the duality thought/language in the perspective of language development. Here are the main findings of his research: at an early stage of linguistic development appears the parallelism of private thought as nonexteriorized or egocentric speech and verbal utterances. That double life of language survives in the adult in the form of inner and exterior speech. Inner speech does not require the grammatical distinction of verbs, modifiers, and nouns; it does not worry about objective references, and it uses fewer words than uttered speech: a noun, an adverb, an adjective can stand alone and suggests a full, complex, and entire semantic field. Vygotsky states that "a single word is so saturated with sense that many words will be required to explain it in external speech," (p. 148) and he concludes that "Inner speech is to a large extent thinking in pure meaning" (p. 149).

Let us pay tribute to this laudable effort to analyze the characteristics of inner speech. I regret only that its philosophical implications are based upon a psychological realism and on the duality of thought and language. Mind is supposed to have its own unexpressed nonreferential language, made of pure meaning, so that the duality thought/language is specified by that of meaning/reference, with this disputable consequence: meaning can exist without referential implication. I shall discuss this crucial issue later. In the meanwhile, it is enough to see that Vygotsky connects the duality meaning/reference with the hypothesis of the psy-referent; and the description of linguistic virtualities tends to call for a psychologistic attitude. If we try to stay in the psycho-linguistic field, we are not authorized to posit the existence of "pure meaning" to explain the existence of those semantic feelings condensed in words not yet grammaticalized. Inner speech is on the one hand a low voice, analogous to theatrical asides, and on the other hand, imagination of language, reverie at its beginnings. Then, the duality between the so-called inner speech and verbal utterance finds its real signification. One can understand why the former is felt to be more extended and richer in meaning than uttered language. The rules of communication require verbal simplification and limitation. The imagination of language feels itself diminished, impoverished. Thus, the accusations against language become an important part of our actualized speech. They go from the daily worries about our verbal utterances ("Don't misunderstand me," "what I mean is," "I cannot tell you how . . . ," the American "you know what I mean," and many other phrases that correct our performances on behalf of an imaginary language) to love letters apologizing for their emotional inadequacy, to laments or revolts of the poets, to the mysticism of the ineffable, or to the linguistic skepticism and pessimism of Beckett's *The Unnamable* and its last phrases between silence and loudness: "perhaps it's a dream, [. . .] a dream silence, full of murmurs, I don't know, that's all words [. . .] that's all I know . . . perhaps they have said me already [. . .] in the silence you don't know . . . "[14] Far from being out of the referential exigency, as Vygotsky thinks, this is inner speech as preliminary imagination of language, experiencing the double feeling of linguistic exhilaration and depression toward references, in confrontation with exterior speech.

In light of those remarks, the Chomskyan distinction should be refined and revised. *Competence,* as universal grammar, designates certain neurophysiological dispositions of the human brain, as common to the human race; it receives different interpretations in the so-called natural languages. *Performance* is the expression of that competence. The existence of "inner speech" shows that human linguistic experiences cannot be reduced to the causal passage from an implicit essence (i.e., competence) to its modes of actualization (performance). In its performances language is not a collective being. It is intersubjective and, originally, the act of an individual. Surely, the latter's inherited brain is his competence, both universal and personal. Common experience shows that the individuals practicing a given tongue are not equally bright. There are two basic gifts, that concerning a special competence, and that of learning a language in its synchronic and diachronic particularities. Let us consider only the gift of individual competence. It is a direct consciousness of language, a linguistic reflexivity: I am linguistically competent *and* I know it. The 'and' has no chronological meaning. My competence is also my knowledge. Such is the origin of inner speech for everybody. We can even infer that the 'inner speech' in its daily manifestations is all the more rich as the gift of competence is more original. Then, between competence and performance, there is a state of language that is interior language—performance not submitted to the laws of communication but indirectly and paradoxically expressed in the exterior utterances of literary reveries of all sorts. The Chomskyan model can be improved this way: *competence-interior performance-exterior performance,* with the understanding that competence is in itself an abstract being, conveniently established for the study of universal grammar but that the linguistic experience proper is exclusively performance as linguistic consciousness and dialectical relation between a reflection and a projection. By 'dialectical' I mean that one can radicalize the linguistic duality of interior and exterior in order to avoid any slip toward the psy-referent. There is no experimental proof that language goes from inside to outside, from conscious performance to performance achieved. This is probably why the polemics between Chomsky and Skinner's supporters is endless, if not useless. Language consciousness or inner speech can serve as a preliminary and preparatory phase for full utterances; but it is also control of utterance and protest against it. Sometimes it is repressed utterance. If I call upon the Saussurian opposition, I say that inner and exterior speeches coexist simultaneously in a dynamic of interaction, synchronic and diachronic within a total experience.

*Meditating on the three pairs "interior/exterior, reflecting/reflected, visible/invisible" with the help of literary reveries.* Exploring the implications behind any form of such modern idealisms as epistemologies or metaphysics of the Subject, we constantly came across three antinomical pairs that engage in the ontological leap out of language: *interior/exterior, invisible/visible, reflecting/reflected.* Needless to say, they overlap and form a dual system: "interior-reflecting-invisible," opposed to "exterior-reflected-visible," the first group referring to the subjective world of consciousness, the second to the objective world. Here is our new problem: *is it possible to forget those ontological transfers, to contain the three pairs within the limits of an exclusive linguistic status, and to admit that they belong uniquely to the nature of language, as modes of its existence?*

When philosophers or poets praise the value of intimacy and make of interior life the highest degree of human experience, they may describe the invisible world of the psy-referent at its most reflective tension; but I can decide to avoid the hypothetical onus of an ontological option and can declare that those people need to promote a language entailing a certain lifestyle, opposed, for instance, to the objective language of science and to its economic consequences in a consumer society: interiority then designates a *value* immanent to the life of language that affects the other types of life that form a human culture. Interiority is a chance language offers to individuals: Jean-Jacques Rousseau's *Rêveries du promeneur solitaire* refer to actual reveries during walks in the country, reveries that reached literary expression, which in its turn proposes to readers a new language and a new lifestyle. To extol interior life is to maintain the superiority of a kind of psy-language over an objective language referred to visible and external objects. I can experience the complex aspects of a language devoted to reflective processes and values of interior life without believing in the existence of an interior world hypothetically made of feelings and ideas. Even when I say or write "my interior feelings are untranslatable into words," I am making a language adjustment; I am enjoying that statement in its full meaning. It does not prove that I have access to "my feelings" as if I were entering a very special room in my house and finding objects I could not perceive before. Indeed, it is true that I can be a liar or a fake; I say that phrase to impress my partners in conversation, when I feel nothing at all. Then, one will say: "your words are only words, not reality." Again, this ontological call does not push us out of language. It merely makes a distinction between two kinds of language, two qualities of reference, two degrees of commitments.

Here is another instance. Let us meditate on Heraclitus's assertion that "Invisible harmony is worth more than visible harmony." Visible harmony designates any sort of harmony perceived through our senses, and with a prevalence of visual experience. Heraclitus's aphorism implies another expression: "Interior or spiritual harmony is worth more than exterior and perceived harmony." The opposition of the visible and invisible becomes that of mind and body. To what is "invisible harmony" referring? It is a negative referential indication; it is beyond what is visible or audible. I feel the harmony of this or that landscape, of that architectural composition, of that melody, even of that perfume; but, at the same time, I feel something else, as if that mountain, that place, that sonata were referring to another world beyond our sensorial grasp. I can make the same remark for a poem, contrasting the perceptible harmony of words with the secret harmony of an inaudible music. I feel as if there should be a referent other than the one I imagine through my senses. Furthermore, why do we insist on the visual experience and its invisible contrary? Do we transpose into meaning the opposition of transparency and opacity, of light and obscurity? It is difficult to understand how a pure visual experience, if it ever exists in normal life, can lead to the consciousness of something extravisual. The feeling of invisible reality, when it goes beyond the relativity of visual indexation, is really a linguistic experience and, more precisely, the experience of a language reflecting upon a sensorial experience within language itself. In consequence, the belief in invisible harmony is not referential illusion, not even the only negative experience of the limits of the visible. It is the strong and positive feeling that *the language of the visible harmony is itself beyond the actual visible harmony*. The duality of language and visual experience is then transposed into the arbitrary duality of two worlds.

Let me imagine myself in front of a painting at the Louvre Museum, let it be Delacroix's *Dante in Hell*. What is my visual experience? It is global and particular, a quick oscillation going from the global perception of the painting to its many details. Is it purely visual? Obviously not! If I am alone, I am conscious of an effort to develop an inner speech as long as I stay in front of the painting: actually seeing is a condensed, unexpressed language remaining a disposable memory that I can try to formulate in speech or writing at any other time. If I were a painter, I would keep in addition the memory, not of a specific organization of forms and colors but of their organization by the movement of brushes that made the original painting. It would be the same situation for a musician listening to a sonata or even an actor to a poem. If my analysis is correct, a painting seen, a sonata performed, or a poem recited are simultaneously invitations to be repeated and to be translated into languages. They constitute a double dynamic and linguistic experience. Thus, the "invisible" can suggest imaginations, which are themselves linguistically performed; for example, in the form of the following statement, "I cannot help feeling the presence of God when looking at the play of light of a sunset on the slopes of those hills as it goes softly down toward the long shades of the valley below." To speak of the invisible beauty of nature is at the same time to recognize the omnipresence of language in human life and to confess immediately its own limits. The invisible becomes a metaphor for the unnamable; *it names the unnamable*. After all, is it not the essence of language? Delacroix wrote: "La pensée fait le langage en se faisant par le langage." [Making itself by language, thought makes language.] This sentence reveals the best effort to translate an experience maintaining the duality of thought and language, saying that there is no thought out of language, and thought is the power of language. It can be applied to the Heraclitean aphorism: "Making itself by the invisible, the visible makes the invisible."

References to the *unknown* are a similar way of staying within language while pretending to be out of it. I found a remarkable analysis of the Unknown in Henry James's "The Art of the Novel." Thinking over the fact that neither the nature of man's faculty nor the nature of his experience has ever quite determined the imagination of great novelists such as Scott, Balzac, or Zola, he opens a parenthesis and meditates on the notion of "romantic":

> I suggest not that the strange and the far are at all necessarily romantic: they happen to be simply unknown, which is quite a different matter. The real represents to my perception the things we cannot possibly *not* know, sooner or later, in one way or another; it being but one of the accidents of our hampered state, and one of the incidents of their quantity and number, that particular instances have not yet come our way. The romantic stands, on the other hand, for the things that, with all the facilities in the world, all the wealth and all the courage and all the will and all the adventure, we never can directly know: the things that can reach us only through the beautiful circuit of our thought and our desire.[15]

That is a penetrating, idealist analysis, implying a parallel distinction of two sorts of invisible-unknown and a call for the psy-referent as thought and desire, but the true Jamesian solution relies on the difference between two knowledges and two unknown things: the first, of scientific type with the help of the categories of quantity and numbers; the second, of artistic type and indirectly through the imagination of the poet, of the novelist and, more generally, of the artist. The hypothesis of the psy-referent is not necessary to James's view. His analysis would remain the same if he had said at the end: "through the beautiful circuit of writing or of any artistic process seen as powers of imaginary creation." Indeed, I am conscious of an important implication concerning the analogy of language and art processes. It would require an exhaustive elaboration around the reflective pair "language of art/art of language." Meanwhile, we can see how the psy-referent appears unnecessary for the experience of the invisible unknown. It suffices for our present meditation.

The third category of subjectivity—that of *reflexivity* at the heart of the Cartesian *Cogito*—is heralded as the psychological experience par excellence and at the same time recognized by linguists as one of the universal properties of language, although very little has been done to confront those two varieties of reflection. One commonly admits that linguistic reflexivity is the consequence of the reflexivity of the psy-referent. Thus, the true problem is to understand what I mean when upon being asked what I am doing, I answer: "I am reflecting." (The French comes more naturally: "Je réfléchis," as synonym of "I am thinking.") By that phrase I mean that without speaking aloud or writing, sometimes with my eyes closed and my head slightly bent, I am ruminating some idea in my head or I am dreaming around some intuition or feeling, I am meditating and making of the world a room—my room—I am scouring. All those words turn around a central one, that of *coiling* as dominant image of interior life. We come back to our analysis of the category of interiority, with nothing to add to our former conclusion: "reflecting" is a possible way of language favoring interiority as a value, and consequently, leading to a paradoxical vocal language of interior life, which is the source of all literary forms.

When Descartes writes: "I doubt, I am", he means much more than the literal meaning of the phrase, in order to justify his ontological leap. "I doubt" is a mode of "I think." I write 'I' because there is no thought-in-general (*cogitatum*), just an individual, subjective reality which is thinking, one way or another (*Cogito*). However, at the very instant I write "I doubt," I think I doubt, I refer to the preceding moment when I was doubting; maybe am I writing to recapture in one instant all my reasons for denying the existence of the external world and the possibility of truth. As is well known, it is the very moment I realize I am asserting myself as doubting. It is not exactly "I exist because I doubt," but immediately "When I become conscious of my doubting, I become conscious of my existence; I feel myself existing in doubting: I am introducing my consciousness as reflective power." "I doubt" means "I think that I doubt," and finally "I think that I think." The first 'think' is rather simple in its understanding: I posit a certain activity at the moment it manifests itself, and I call it 'reflection' to underline the property of consciousness. What do I mean by 'thinking'? If we follow Descartes' suggestion, I mean "understanding" (in French *entendement*) as power of intuition and deduction. Intuition refers to two aspects of thinking—having ideas, being conscious of them (for instance, the innate ideas of space, time, number, infinite, etc.). I don't necessarily have some idea of belief in my mind. I just refer to a possibility or a memory of thinking. The only act of thinking (if I may say so) is the thinking that I am thinking, even if I have no specific thought under my attention.

Thus, I mean no more than "I am writing." When I write the famous Cartesian phrase, I just affirm a permanent power of reduplication limited to my experience of language, because I cannot write "I walk that I walk." When I apply reduplication to psy-words other than 'thought' or its equivalents, I am saying more than reduplicating the fact of thinking. For instance, "I think that I believe" or "I will that I will" or "I remember that

I remember." In those cases reduplication adds a new meaning to "I believe, I will, I remember, etc.," whence "I think that I think" is supposed to add nothing to "I think" except for extolling the implication that *any linguistic expression is reflective.*

Descartes' followers divided themselves between those who believed in innate ideas and those who denied the existence of such ideas. Each group, however, kept the basic belief in a psy-referent, and worked hard at creating *languages of consciousness,* be they called *Essay on Human Understanding, Treatise of Human Nature, Essai sur l'origine des connaissances, Kritik der Reinen Vernunft, Phenomenologie des Geistes,* and so on. All those essays were enormous uncoilings of "I think that I think"; they felt themselves as auto-descriptions and auto-justifications of a psy-referent that made of language the more or less faithful servant of human or divine minds.

During the same period, preromantic, romantic and symbolist writers exalted the reflective power of consciousness. Again and again they were obsessed by the double scheme of the window and the mirror, closely linked to the discovery of reverie's powers, and the promotion of interior life. The window, as invitation to the invisible, is by itself a call for the games of reflection. It leads to the idealization of the psy-referent that is transfused into a pure world of ideal essences. Mallarmé's "Les Fenêtres" gives the best illustration of the conversion of transparency into reflexivity:

> Je fuis et je m'attache à toutes les croisées
> D'où l'on tourne l'épaule à la vie, et, béni,
> Dans leur verre, lavé d'éternelles rosées,
> Que dore le matin chaste de l'Infini.
>
> Je me mire et me vois Ange! et je meurs, et j'aime
> —Que la vitre soit l'art, soit la mysticité—
> A renaître, portant mon rêve en diadème,
> Au ciel antérieur où fleurit la Beauté![16]

(My translations do not intend to be "literary"; they are deliberately literal and only hope to maintain in another language the references looked for by the quoted writers.)

> [I flee and I tarry at all the windows
> From which one turns one's shoulders to life, and, blessed,
> Washed by eternal dews in their glass,
> Gilded by the chaste morning of Infinite.

I look at myself and see myself as an Angel! I die, and I love
—may the windowpane be Art, mysticism!—
Being born again, wearing my dream like a diadem,
In the preexisting heaven where Beauty is blooming!]

This poem, with its Platonic overtones, its glass mirror, and its mixing of flashes and reflected light, refers to Baudelaire's great poems and proses, to "Bénédiction," for example, of which the final stanza is so suggestive:

Car il [the 'diadème,' symbol of ideal Beauty] ne sera fait que de pure lumière,
Puisée au foyer saint des rayons primitifs,
Et dont les yeux mortels, dans leur splendeur entière,
Ne sont que des miroirs obscurcis et plaintifs!

[Because it will be made of pure light only,
Drawn from the holy hearth of primitive beams,
And of which mortal eyes, in their full splendor,
Are but darkened and plaintive mirrors!][17]

In *Les Fleurs du Mal* as well as in *Le Spleen de Paris*, the *eye* is the miraculous encounter of the window and the mirror, the alchemic crucible ('creuset') where the light is at once source and reflection, movement inward and movement outward. It is as if the poet were living the diverse experiments of sensory consciousness, especially those relative to visual sensations, feeling through them the pervading presence of another world: sight is vision-and-reflection, and thus, as the sensorial approximation of a spiritual experience, offers the most direct access to it. Here are a few samples of the Baudelairian visual experience between transparency and opacity and its double thematic of plate glass and mirror. In *Poèmes en prose:* "Il n'est pas d'objet plus profond, plus mystérieux, plus fécond, plus ténébreux, plus éblouissant qu'une fenêtre éclairée d'une chandelle" ("Les Fenêtres") [There is no object deeper, more mysterious, more fecund, more obscure, more dazzling than a window lighted by a candle],[18] and this enigmatic question:

Un homme épouvantable entre et se regarde dans la glace.
— Pourquoi vous regardez-vous au miroir, puisque vous ne pouvez vous y voir qu'avec déplaisir? L'homme épouvantable me répond:
— . . . je possède le droit de me mirer." ("Le miroir")

[A frightful-looking man enters and looks at himself in a mirror.
— Why do you look at yourself in a mirror, since you can only see yourself with displeasure? The frightful-looking man answers me:
— . . . I have the right to look at myself.][19]

In *Les Fleurs du Mal* almost every poem is an experience in vision and reflection, with a permanent nostalgia of the anterior-interior life of the psy-referent:

La mer est ton miroir . . . Tu te plais à plonger au sein de ton image"

[Ocean is your mirror. . . . You enjoy immersing yourself into the heart of your own image]. ("L'Homme et la mer")

Et le soleil, le soir, ruisselant et superbe,
Qui, derrière la vitre où se brisait sa gerbe,
Semblait, grand oeil ouvert dans le ciel curieux,
Contempler nos dîners longs et silencieux,
Répandant largement ses beaux reflets de cierge
Sur la nappe frugale et les rideaux de serge.

[And the sun, in the evening, streaming and superb,
Which behind the glass where its spray was breaking itself,
Looked like a large open eye in the curious heaven
Contemplating our long and silent dinners
Abundantly spreading its beautiful candle-like reflections
On the frugal tablecloth and the serge curtains.] ("Je n'ai pas oublié . . .")

Nos deux coeurs seront deux vastes flambeaux,
Qui réfléchiront leurs doubles lumières
Dans nos deux esprits, ces miroirs jumeaux.

[Our hearts will become two vast torches
Which will reflect their double lights
In our two souls, those twin mirrors.] ("La Mort des amants")

Je ne vois qu'infini par toutes les fenêtres,
Et mon esprit, toujours du vertige hanté
Jalouse du néant l'insensibilité.
Ah! ne jamais sortir des Nombres et des Etres!

[I only see infinity beyond all the windows,
And my mind always haunted by vertigo

Is jealous of Nothingness's insensitivity.
Ah! never to go out of Numbers and Beings!] ("Le Gouffre")

De purs miroirs qui font choses plus belles

[Pure mirrors which make all things more beautiful] ("La Beauté")

"Tu contiens dans ton oeil le couchant et l'amour"

[You hold in your eye sunset and love] ("Hymne à la Beauté")

. . . et n'as-tu pas
Devant tous les miroirs vu pâlir tes appâts?

[Have you not seen in front of all mirrors your charms turning pale?"] ("Tu mettrais l'univers . . . ")

Plonger dans vos beaux yeux comme dans un beau songe

[To immerse oneself into your beautiful eyes as in a beautiful dream] ("Semper eadem")

Je suis le sinistre miroir
Où la mégère se regarde

[I am the sinister mirror in which the shrew looks at herself"] ("Heautontimoroumenos")

Lacs où mon âme tremble et se voit à l'envers

[Lakes in which my soul quivers and sees itself inside out] ("Le Poison")

In his essay on Proust, Samuel Beckett reproaches Baudelaire with his double aspiration to linguistic transparency: Baudelairian symbols, says the future author of *Game's End*, are symbols of something else, whereas Proust understands more perceptively that the literary work can be but symbol of itself. I leave aside the relevance and fairness of that reproach by the poet who likes to say: "There is nothing to express, nothing with which to express, nothing from which to express, no power to express, no desire to express, together with the obligation to express." However, for our own purpose and meditative experiment, it is enough to observe that Baudelaire's poetry is the opposite of a poetic evasion. It looks for a double anchoring in the Sensible and the Unknown, neither leading to the other but one lived through the other. Poetry, then, would be a double invitation to the forgetfulness of language by itself and to the remembrance of the soul through the mediation of sensations. Shall we conclude that, for poets like Baudelaire, who intensely live the triple experience of language—interiority, invisibility, reflectivity—in literary reveries, the belief in a dual psy-referent of senses and soul seems inevitable?

Poetry, even in the hands of its most lucid exponents, although it superbly illustrates the belief in a psy-referent, is unable to explain and justify its existence. One could even say that Poetry, better than psychology itself, explores the rich virtualities of the belief in a psy-referent. It is probable that from the beginnings of human histories, Poetry, long an accessory to religion, helped to entertain complex semantic systems of the mind and to cultivate the vision of transparent universes of representations. I would not hesitate to risk the idea that poetry, read in transparency, is the main laboratory for the entertaining of the psy-referent. However, that cultural and linguistic experiment will never prove that the psy-referent is a being independent of Poetry or is cause of Poetry. Far from it! One should even reverse the evidence exalted by the *Cogito:* instead of saying that the psy-referent is the foundation of Poetry, should not we state that Poetry is the existential support of the psy-referent? Poetry itself is made of such a paradox: a mirroring moment between itself and the Soul as referent. *Les Fleurs du Mal* grow from that paradox: Beauty makes poems exist and, through them, the Soul emerges. In any of Baudelaire's poems, there is double awareness of the nostalgic and attractive power of the referent and of the immediate, alchemic power of poetry. "L'Invitation au voyage" is actually invitation to poetry and poetry of invitation.

Our analysis is no longer progressing. We can only conclude that, no more than philosophy, poetry has not helped us to justify the belief in the existence of a psy-referent, although it has confirmed that such a belief is as anchored in any human culture as that of the existence of an external world. Then is it not ridiculous to resist such natural inclination, even if we cannot offer better proofs than that of their natural acceptance, with the exception of a few odd thinkers? There is a deep difference between the philosopher and the poet, at least when the later does not pretend to be also a philosopher who enunciates the pros and cons of metaphysical propositions. By itself the poem is linguistic realization. It does not speak on behalf of God or a spiritual world; it speaks on behalf of Poetry as ultimate expression of language. It does not describe an independent referent as philosophers speaking of Nature. Poetry exposes the referential power of language for itself, and it does not mean that its productions imply the existence of a psy-referent. To call a poet "realist" or "idealist" is to stop seeing in him or her a poet, and to read his or her work as ontological information.

Now, with this difference in mind, let us try a reverse Berkeleyan gesture: instead of opening the curtain of words, but at the same time continuing to produce chains of words, let us draw aside the curtain of the psy-referent, the *psychological curtain*. We have noted that there is no sensorial or extrasensorial experience per se, none referring to a psychological state of mind, nor to a state of matter. The subject-object relation cannot be based upon its extralinguistic origin. The concept of causality is applicable within a field of knowledge, never to trespass it. Logically, physically, psychologically, one will never show how the power of the mind creates language, if not at the price of vicious circles surreptitiously making prelinguistic conditions of logical, physical, psychological ones. Finally one arrives at the strange situation of dividing language into two independent parts, one physical, the other psychological, or, at the limit, of differenciating two kinds of biological conditions—that of the brain and that of the rest of the body; for example, the different organs contributing to the vocal emission of a linguistic sign could be put in a linear chain of causality—first some part of the brain, then the pharynx, then the throat, the tongue, the lips.

Let us come back to the metaphor of opening the psychological curtain. It is a metaphor—an experiment. Its effect is to nullify the reference to psychological states, to fight the common sense of linguistic transparency in order to feel the presence of words in a total experience of language and ultimately to become aware that any psychological reference does not necessarily imply a psy-referent. "Drawing the curtain" reinforces the metaphor of "uncapping." Both help meditation to extricate itself from the belief in the three antinomies of the visible/invisible, the exterior/interior, and the reflecting/reflected, and to reinstate them in the life of language. We know that it is not an easy stand, and there are many linguistic relapses and hidden spiritual debauches. However, with patience, with repeated exercises, which take subjects and objects back toward their original linguistic processes, little by little, meditation affirms its vocation of universal uncapping; and it learns to play the subtle game of the same and the other, of presence and absence within the life of language, within the progressive and elusive attempts to make oneself indefinite word islands.

To finish with those efforts to make our own writing conscious of its *writing immediacy,* that is, to remind meditation that it meditates on meditation and does not require the distinctive existence of a psy-referent, let us consider one of Paul Valéry's elegant and enigmatic witticisms: "Voir c'est oublier le nom de la chose que l'on voit" [To see is to forget the name of the thing one sees]. Indeed, it is the saying of a poet who is first aware of words and is anxious to give to his lines an ontological weight, be it sensorial or spiritual. 'Voir' is ambivalent: it designates the double contemplation of an existence and an essence; it suggests a double hope of being able to surpass language: I can lose my self, Berkeley or Condillac style, in the sensation itself, and say "I am the rose's smell" or, Plato style, in the vision of the Idea of rose. Not being a philosopher more or less abiding logic, Valéry plays on the chance of the double pleasure that language seeks to obtain, the pleasures of concreteness and abstraction. However, when he says that the forgetfulness of a word *is* vision, he does not claim that drawing the curtain, according to Berkeley or Plato's moods, is an actual psychological operation. Far from it, he refers to the case of linguistic memory and to a special experiment where the absence of words means vision. More than anything else he enjoys his witticism, which is a brilliant way of understanding that a word is a double power of absence and presence, and its momentary absence is language absorbing itself into sensation or insight. If there is psychological reference here, it is within language. In a very French way, like a ballerina on her toes, Valéry changes spirit into wit; in French it would be said that "l'esprit du mot devient le mot d'esprit" [the spirit of the word becomes witticism], implying that Poetry is a superior witticism.

Valéry's phrase can be understood in its literal meaning. In daily life there are examples of vision combined with the forgetfulness of a word: for example, I often say, "I see her face as if she were in front of me, but I cannot remember her name." Such a situation can happen with common names: "I can picture that tool, and I am unable to remember its name." Is it not the clear demonstration of a hiatus that separates perception and language? I reserve for other meditations a full examination of the duality of perception and language. For the moment let us observe that such an experience can be understood within the limits of the linguistic memory process thanks to which words appear in my speaking or writing with a group of connotations. It happens that connotations are remembered before or without the name I am looking for. I do not remember the name of Mrs. Smith, but I am able to describe her face or her figure. I can say,

"Please tell me the name of the author of *Oblomov,* it has slipped my mind." Three centuries of psychological modeling have imposed on us a pattern describing such failures, but all of them are based on the ontological leap, which is in itself a linguistic operation. *The fact that language seems to make a jump does not prove that its presuppositions of a process entails the reality of a psy-referent.*

*Uncapping human sciences.* Here we are again at the same moment of ontological uncapping, undecision, and suspense. I have postponed up to now the problem that, I guess, has been in the mind of my reader since the beginning of this third meditation: If we refuse to make a decision on any kind of existential judgment concerning the psy-referent, does it mean that we should cast doubt over all human sciences, whatever their independent object may be, psychology, sociology, history, and their intermediaries, until they can be integrated in physiology? The correct answer should be "yes"! A so-called scientific sociological, psychological, historical statement, when stripped of its mathematical apparatus and reduced to its qualitative vocabulary, does not go beyond the remarks that have been made for centuries by philosophy and literature. For instance, in matters of human emotions or passions, do I learn more by studying a recent treatise of psychology or a dictionary of psychoanalysis instead of David Hume's *Treatise of Human Nature* or Jean-Jacques Rousseau's *Rêveries du promeneur solitaire*? Obviously not!

There is something more serious. It is impossible to decide if that kind of statement is theoretical or practical—the general description of a behavior or a coding system that would permit human beings to speak and to direct their actions. Liberal and Marxist sociologies describe and codify in opposite manners their understanding of democracy; actually they are hidden ethics and languages available for the man on the street who, thanks to them and their mediatic polarizations, coins his own idiolect. Another typical example is that of the French moralists, from Rabelais and Montaigne to Sartre, Camus, and Bataille: their language is halfway between analytical descriptions and moral aspirations, between psychological observations and moral learning. I do not mean to say that the moralists pass from judgments of fact to value judgments and vice-versa. In its own unique movement their discourse is determinative and constitutive. Reading them, even when I challenge them, I learn how to speak about myself and I become able to give to my actions a background of justifications. In other countries, theater and poetry play similar roles and express themselves through that ambiguous language that, at the very moment it refers to some human being, gives and interprets the cipher of his life.

My attempt to uncap human sciences and their diverse conceptions of psy-referents should not lead to blind approval of the imperialistic trend of semiotics, also called semiology. It does not suffice to replace 'being' by 'sign' to solve the problem of the relation between language and reality. Let us reread de Saussure's announcement in *Cours de linguistique générale:*

> A science that studies the life of signs within society is conceivable [. . . .] I shall call it *semiology* (from Greek *sèmeîon* 'sign'). Semiology would show what constitutes signs, what laws govern them. Since the science does not yet exist, no one can say what it would be. But it has a right to existence, a place staked out in advance. Linguistics is only a part of the general science of semiology; the laws discovered by semiology will be applicable to linguistics, and the latter will circumscribe a well-defined area within the mass of anthropological facts.[20]

Today, there is nothing to be said against this project even if, seventy years later, semiotics has been unable to go beyond empirical and descriptive knowledge. However, it should be noticed that it relies on all the presuppositions that scientific realism seems to require for its own success, especially the existence of an object called 'sign' and, among the world of signs, a limited domain called "language." Nothing is said about physiological expectation. Moreover, looking for the implications supporting either the Saussurian or the Peircean definitions of 'sign,' we can detect the postulated presence of the psy-referent, even reduced to the power of producing signs and surrounded by a full ontology of sign with the basic opening proposition, "a sign is a being that is . . . " or, in a more general way, "there is a being called 'sign' that obeys the following laws . . . " At the deep level of meditation the semiotic project does not help to solve the philosophical difficulty we are facing. In my present writing, I have to take measures in order to make the uncapping of the psy-referent more than a purely verbal declaration, a linguistic decision with no consequence for my future writing.

Let me begin by saying-writing that I will no longer believe in the existence of a psy-referent and will never try to introduce it into my discourse. Does this mean that from now on, I will attempt to avoid any kind of use of the psy-vocabulary? If realizable, such a radical purification would be reduced to an arbitrary and superficial physicalism as, I say it once again, the physiology of the brain in its present state cannot authorize a psycho-physiological language leading to the absorption of biology into physics. It is also obvious that I cannot speak about language without calling for words such as "knowledge," "perception," "judgment," "belief," "affirmation," "negation," "reasoning," "impression," "expression," to quote only a few of these lexemes that possess a dubious origin and nationality taken from linguistics, psychology, logic, and rhetoric. I could get around that difficulty by saying that the psy-vocabulary belongs to the domain of psycho-linguistics, and go so far as to state that psychology is a detached part of psycholinguistics. Such a decision would be a return to restoring the semiotic dream and would bring about no significant result for my uncapping enterprise. There is no question of my being seduced by common-sense optimism: I should decide to continue using the psy-vocabulary for practical purposes *but* as if there were no psy-referent. I cannot accept language and condemn it at the same time! I cannot even follow the advice Beckett gives at the end of the *Unnamable:* "where I am, I don't know, I'll never know, in the silence, you don't know, you must go on, I can't go on, I'll go on" without, in his company, falling into the paradoxically proclaimed silent solipsism of one of his last prose poem "Compagnie":

> Jusqu'à ce qu'enfin tu entendes comme quoi les mots touchent à leur fin. Avec chaque mot inane plus près du dernier. Et avec eux la fable. La fable d'un autre avec toi dans le noir. La fable de toi fabulant d'un autre avec toi dans le noir. Et comme quoi mieux vaut tout compte fait peine perdue et toi tel que toujours. Seul.
>
> [Until at last you understand that words reach their limits. With every inane word nearer the last one. And with them the fable. The fable of another in the dark with you. The fable of you telling about another in the dark with you. And insofar it is better after all uselessly and you as such always. Alone.][21]

Refusing the complacent vision of a final scientific state or the moving poetry of silence, I see one only other way—a sort of methodological *sur-nominalism,* that is, a nominalism rejecting the duality between sign and reality. For instance, as a preliminary exercise, I promise to myself that, from this moment on, I will not let the word 'mind' appear in my writing (in such phrases like "I have in mind," "my mind is confused," "you are out of your mind," "that slipped my mind," "I am speaking my mind," etc.) without issuing a warning: "mind is a word, a way of saying; it is not a reality referred to outside my language, and it is not possible to substitute for it the word 'brain.' " However, "it is nothing but a word, a word that could have a meaning and no reference; it does not designate an independent referent, but it has a referential power that it will be my problem to understand, very likely within the frame of a revised notion of language." I should repeat that monologue for any word or phrase belonging to the psy-lexicon and hope that little by little I forget about the secret dream of a hazy or luminous world beyond language and source of language, just knowing that, *if the independent world of mind is an illusion, the experience of mind is real, as an essential part of the life of language within my self.* In that spirit, one day, our future cultures will be able to rewrite and recompose human sciences as we know them.

*Within language, within myself.* In a Cartesian manner, I have to put in balance the two phrases "within language" and "within myself." The *Cogito* tells me that I cannot write the first phrase without writing the second one, so that the psy-referent actually is truly the I-referent. Should I do for 'I' what I just did for 'mind,' and repeat the two parts of the above monologue: " 'I' is a word" but "it is not just a word . . . it has a specific referential power." It means that I should continue to accept the occurrences of 'I'—and how could I do otherwise?—without relying upon the materialist or spiritualist options, not even invoking the dubious privilege of ignorance, not even playing games with the category of Otherness and declaring: "I am other than me, I am other!" Indeed, I am more than a grammatical deictic, although I exist as such. I am more than a reflective reference in a play of mirror, although I understand myself as a reflective power. Then, if I write, "Today I feel the same as I did yesterday," or on the contrary, "I feel different from how I did yesterday," I should be aware that *I* am saying that, and thus the memory of myself as same or different is possible through the continuity of my discourse, and the particularity of 'I' is the particularity of *my* language. It is also true that *my* I is reluctant to be confused with the linguistic performance he or she is responsible for; but this reluctance is part of my linguistic abilities and limitations: "I could say it otherwise," "I could say more than I say." For the moment, and until proven incorrect, I should think that *feeling oneself inside and outside language is to experience and to express an essential linguistic power.* We can imagine a myth of language as the fable of a jail with neither bars nor wardens, where the prisoners are eager to escape and exhaust their lives in planning a great escape that never takes place. If I repeat it to myself every morning, this little fable should contribute to derealizing the psy-referent without entertaining the dream of the illusory escapes proposed by skepticism and solipsism or without falling into the pessimistic view of linguistic formalism. In other words, the basic fight against the psy-referent—and its uncapping, the constant return to the awareness of language each time I have the permanent illusory feeling that I leave it—should be accompanied by the idea that current notions about language should also be revised. Most of the traditional conceptions on language have been set with the backing of classic and modern, psychological, transcendental, and sociological ontologies. If we require the uncapping of those kinds of ontologies in the form of their confessed or implied realisms or idealisms as well as of their theories of the human mind, conversely we should undertake to rectify their complementary philosophies of language. Indeed it should be our most urgent task.

Let us meditate on Wittgenstein's antipsychologism: his rejection of the metaphor of the "mind's eye" and condemnation of the ontology of private life as well as of psychological interiority, will provide a convenient transition. Surely Wittgenstein is right in seeing in "interiority" a mythical construction deriving from a metaphysical transfer of words from familiar language. Along with many people who work today in the field of the "cognitive human sciences,"[22] Wittgenstein considers that human thinking is guided by *rules* that have a formative power and that there is no such thing as a private rule: 'private' takes its meaning not within the individual/social opposition but within the internal/external one. The preceding analysis of exteriority concurs with Wittgenstein's analysis, but it needs a few corrections.

First, if it is true that there is no private rule, for the same and complementary reason there is no public rule per se either. A rule—let us say "to make my videocassette recorder project a film, I must push successively the operator and the play buttons"—is part of the formal structure of an object—in this case the VCR on the table in front of me. The rule exists only when I am aware of it; actually, it is one of my specifications and related to the VCR. I cannot separate a rule from its applications in a given object, and there are infinite ways of applying rules and infinite results in their applications, although social conformity and superficial perception can blunt differences. Moreover, in Wittgenstein's discourse, there are many implications with which I can no longer agree. He seems to accept the myth of natural language as familiar language and thus the good usage of a psy-referent that does not pretend to philosophical or scientific conclusions. Common pragmatism is not far away! Then, one may wonder if a familiar language with philosophical implications exists—surely not technically elaborated philosophical discourses but a sort of often untold, although ready-to-be-explicited, familiar philosophy. I am afraid that Wittgenstein's idea of familiar language is as mythical as the philosophical psy-language he rightly censures. Finally, behind that "public" familiar and practical language made of rules and their applications, we can guess the presence of one of the most insidious presuppositions with which we have not yet been confronted but that we have shamelessly used: *language is an instrument to play with.*

MEDITATION FOUR

# *Uncapping the Instrumental Way of Thinking: The Pervading Forms of Pragmatic Modernism and the F-Function*

### *Lexical and Semantic Awareness*

Let us begin by surveying the language that qualifies beings as functions (I will call it F-language) with the aid of dictionaries and our own experience, but without claiming to build up an artificial system of internal and external lexical derivation.

'Instrumentality' can qualify a screwdriver or a spacecraft. It designates an object or a group of objects fabricated for a certain purpose in view of being used. Any object can be changed into an instrument when integrated into any sort of action. The tree I see can serve as escape from a barking dog or as the means of seeing a broader horizon. Each part of an instrument—real or potential—is dependent on the other parts; and in its unity, it is dependent on the world at large understood as opened instrumentality. Two qualifications are in order: the instrument is *subservient* (to an end) and *prospective* (it initiates a spatio-temporal situation). Instrumentality splits into three lexical forms: *instrument, utility, function,* with their numerous synonyms, or said in another way, *form, use, end,* so that instrumentality-thinking implies a kind of Leibniziam *Principle of Sufficient Reason:* any being has a reason for existing as it is (realist reading), or any being is understood as an objective or subjective form with an actual or potential use determined by an internal or external end (idealist reading). Needless to say, these phrasings constitute a knot of philosophical problems.

Looking in Roget's *Thesaurus,* I observe that 'instrumentality' covers the universal field of 'action' within a square, the four corners of which are 'causation, motion, intellect, volition.' Interestingly enough, this square dominates five or six categories in Roget's tabular synopsis of categories. The one left out is the class of 'affections.' One could be surprised by this exclusion: for instance, a smile, a tear, have strong instrumental powers. They do, but their expressions, the passage from affection to action, are usable and do not concern the emotion or feeling behind. Anyway, it is a problem that should not be forgotten. For the moment let us keep in mind that, if instrumentality invades the territory of affections, it does so through the intermediary of mental or physical actions.

The lexical quasi-omnipresence of instrumentality comes from its close connection to the world and the thought of action. It commonly implies a reference to the world and to the human mind, or any other mind (for instance, in theology and in psychobiology). It also applies to language immediately understood as a general aspect of human action. Normally, without philosophical sophistications, a sign in the state of being used is grasped as an instrument: smoke is an effect of fire; 'smoke' is a sign; 'smoke' becomes an instrument of demonstration in a given action (to fight a fire, to be an example in a discussion). The states of object, sign, and instrument are inseparable in daily life and in the daily use of language.

J. D. Ross argues that the underlying structure of all propositions describing activities contains a highest predicate of intentionality whose philological realization in English is 'do'.[1] He is right: thus 'to be' is not clearly distinct from 'to do'; and the intentionality of doing calls for the functionality of making: being is understood as a doing that entails a making. There is a permanent circulation between 'to be,' 'to do,' and 'to make,' and finally, between 'to use,' 'to be at use,' 'to be in use' for any sort of referent, and, more typically, for language itself. When aware of itself, language simultaneously qualifies itself as being, object, subject, action, sign, instrument, and utility. If I say, "I was born in Autun, France," I make this statement for a definite purpose; in itself it is a 'description,' a sort of linguistic action made possible by grammatical and semantic functions, and my sentence is a combination of instrumentality forms. If I say, "Are you coming with me to the library?," 'coming' is not descriptive; it designates a potential action; it is thus instrumentality for the planned action. When I tell a nonsense story, I am looking for a certain comic effect; I am conscious of the story as the instrument of my intention. There is no need to add examples. The same conclusion would be forced upon us. Whatever I say, when experiencing language, I treat it as a potential or effective instrument. When I write ". . . therefore I am," I act, I use my language to act, or act to use my language; I am conscious of it as a useful, efficient instrument.

To sum up, reading Roget's *Thesaurus*'s enterprise of lexical classification, or interrogating my simplest experience of language, I come to this statement: ***language-usage constitutes a permanent semantic permutation between the categories of being, doing, making, using, inside references to the physical world, to the mind, and to myself.*** I propose to call F-function and F-language the varied expressions of language usage.

## *Linguistics' Common Implication of the F-Function*

At the beginning of their descriptive or constructive approaches, linguists do not hesitate to call for the F-language, most of them in a very "natural" way and without explicit comment. For instance, André Martinet, in *Eléments de linguistique générale,* declares "l'essentielle fonction de cet instrument qu'est une langue est celle de communication" [the essential function of this instrument that is a language is that of communication][2] and "chaque langue est une organisation participant des données de l'expérience" [each language is an organization based upon empirical data][3]; the key words of function, instrument, and organization, occur as undefined prerequisites. Michel Bréal, in *Essai de sémantique,* recognizes in language "le plus nécessaire instrument de civilisation" [the most necessary instrument of civilization][4]; later he speaks of the "simplicité des moyens" [simplicity of means] thanks to which language succeeds in being understood. In his chapter on "Analogy," de Saussure makes of analogy the principle of creation of language; he sees in it "une manifestation de l'activité générale qui distingue les unités pour les utiliser ensuite" [a manifestation of the general activity which differentiates the units in order to utilize them later].[5] Is not such a phrase a direct product of the F-language? In the presentation of *Language and Mind,* Chomsky states: "I believe and try to show in these essays, that the study of language structure reveals properties of mind that underlie the exercise of human mental capacities in normal activities, such as the use of language in the ordinary free and creative fashion."[6] It is undeniable that the words 'property', 'exercise', 'capacity', 'activity', 'use,' associated with the same semantic composition belong to the F-language.

There is no need to add other examples. The presence of elements of the F-language seems inevitable in the preliminary steps of linguistic studies. It is well known that the frontiers between grammar, semantics, and pragmatics are constantly and surreptitiously overstepped. There is a great temptation to name "pragmatics" the discipline that gives the different parts of linguistics their ultimate and secret unity. In any case, linguists believe that their scientific enterprise is rooted in ordinary language, and their definitions spring forth from an undefined and inescapable stuff where we just noticed the omnipresence of the F-language. However, linguists' current resignation to preliminary undefined concepts does not suit philosophers who aspire to full explicitation and who thus have to usher in the different categories of language in proper order and language itself in regard to the general referents of world and mind.

## *Descartes' Language Instrumentalism*

Thinking over almost three centuries of philosophy speculation from present perspective, I identify two main phases: the first one where language is subordinated to the psy-referent and understood as *instrument of thought,* the second one where, from the beginning of the nineteenth century on, the F-function tends to overcome and take possession of the ontological language so that philosophy becomes a F-function's systematization, ordinarily called philosophy of action or *practical philosophy*.

For the first phase, Descartes again serves as model—a paradoxical model indeed, as references to language in Descartes' works and letters are scarce, marginal, and as they repeat what he wrote at the end of the fifth part of the *Discourse on Method,* a portion I quote in its entirety:

> Or, par ces deux mêmes moyens, on peut aussi connaître la différence qui est entre les hommes et les bêtes. Car c'est une chose bien remarquable, qu'il n'y a point d'hommes si hébétés et si stupides, sans en excepter même les plus insensés, qu'ils ne soient capables d'arranger ensemble diverses paroles, et d'en composer un discours par lequel ils fassent entendre leurs pensées; et qu'au contraire, il n'y a pas d'autre animal, tant parfait et tant heureusement né qu'il puisse être, qui fasse le semblable. Ce qui n'arrive pas de ce qu'ils ont faute d'organes, car on voit que les pies et les perroquets peuvent proférer des paroles ainsi que nous, et toutefois ne peuvent parler ainsi que nous, c'est-à-dire en témoignant qu'ils pensent ce qu'ils disent; au lieu que les hommes qui, étant nés sourds et muets, sont privés d'organes qui servent aux autres pour parler, autant ou plus que les bêtes, ont coutume d'inventer eux-mêmes quelques signes, par lesquels ils se font entendre à ceux qui, étant ordinairement avec eux, ont loisir d'apprendre leur langue . . . Et on ne doit pas confondre les paroles avec les

> mouvements naturels, qui témoignent les passions et peuvent être imités par des machines aussi bien que par les animaux, ni penser, comme quelques Anciens, que les bêtes parlent, bien que nous n'entendions pas leur language, car s'il était vrai, puisqu'elles ont plusieurs organes qui se rapportent aux nôtres, elles pourraient aussi bien se faire entendre à nous qu'à leurs semblables.
>
> [By these two methods we may also recognize the difference that exists between men and brutes. For it is a very remarkable fact that there are none so depraved and stupid, without even excepting idiots, that they cannot arrange different words together, forming of them a statement by which they make known their thoughts, while, on the other hand, there is no other animal, however perfect and fortunately circumstanced it may be, which can do the same. It is not the want of organs that brings this to pass, for it is evident that magpies and parrots are able to utter words just like ourselves, and yet they cannot speak as we do, that is, so as to give evidence that they think of what they say. On the other hand, men who, being born deaf and dumb, are in the same degree, or even more than the brutes, destitute of the organs which serve the others for talking, are in the habit of themselves inventing certain signs by which they make themselves understood by those who, being usually in their company, have leisure to learn their language. . . . And we ought not to confound words with natural movements which betray passions and may be imitated by machines as well as be manifested by animals; nor must we think, as did some of the Ancients, that brutes talk, although we do not understand their language. For if this were true, since they have many organs which are allied to our own, they could communicate their thoughts to us just as easily as to those of their own race.][7]

Descartes approaches the problem of language in a very indirect way, as an argument in his distinction between humanity and animality, between mind and machine. Animals are machines, they do not speak. Consequently, language is not produced by biological organs, since animals have similar organs, but by our mind. Language has two functions: "arranger ensemble diverses paroles" and "en composer un discours par lequel ils fassent entendre leurs pensées," that is, a grammatical and a semantic function, and a pragmatic function of communication. Following Cartesian dualism, it should be said that pure thinking as well as pure matter are without language, which belongs to the mysterious "unity of mind and body," which is a decision made by God and remains unexplained to man. Language is the invention of man's mind but as a divine gift and with the help of some body organs. Reflecting the intelligible order of the mind, it serves as communication with other minds, through their own bodies. It is an instrument without which human minds would remain isolated in the prison of their bodies. In order to be communicated, words, in their material arrangement and composition, must reproduce the pure light of the mind, existing by itself, independent of the body. Thus language has the double function of thought reproduction and communication. It is a unique and obscure privilege granted to man by God: communication is established between minds but requires the physical world's intervention. Language is thus created and developed in the shadow of human mind's life.

In the same spirit the Port-Royal's *Grammaire générale et raisonnée* opens on the statement that, "Parler, est expliquer ses pensées par des signes que les hommes ont inventés à ce dessein." [To speak is to explain one's thoughts by signs that men invented for that purpose.] Sign is then a mixed being, material and spiritual. Language is the instrument of explication by signs, and grammar is under the control of logic that is the normative theory of the psy-referent. John Locke also remains Cartesian in his general understanding of language: for him, language is the easiest and shortest means of communication; it is "the great instrument and common Tye in Society." In the introduction to the *Essai sur l'origine des connaissances humaines,* Condillac praises Locke for being the first philosopher to write on the problem of words, but says that he (Condillac) plans to go further along the same path, because "je suis convaincu que l'usage des signes est le principe qui développe le germe de toutes nos idées." [I am convinced that the use of signs is the principle which develops the seed of all our ideas.][8] Thus, Condillac remains a dualist: language is an instrument—a method—for the development of our ideas, which in themselves are not signs, but clear or confused visions. More specifically, in Section IV of the *Essai* he analyzes *"l'opération par laquelle nous donnons des signes à nos idées"* [that operation by which we give signs to our ideas]:

> Cette opération résulte de l'imagination qui présente à l'esprit des signes dont on n'avait point encore l'usage et de l'attention qui les lie avec les idées: elle est une des plus essentielles dans la recherche de la vérité; cependant elle est une des moins connues.
>
> [That operation comes from imagination which presents to the mind signs the usage of which one did not know yet and from attention which ties them with ideas: it is one of the most essential in the search for truth; however, it is one of the less known.][9]

This text results from the combination of two juxtaposed languages—the languages of the psy-referent (imagination, attention, idée, esprit) and of the F-function (opération, signe, usage). Language is the instrument—Condillac calls it "analyse"—that gives to human mind the necessary means to develop his ideas into the logical order of Truth. Then, beyond Locke, Condillac comes closer to the idea of converting the language of the psy-referent into that of the F-function because any psychological operation cannot achieve its full expression without the intervention of signs. He never makes the definite jump: for him, language is instrument *of* thought—instrument *for* thought in the human condition after the Fall:

> Ainsi il ne s'agit pas de considérer l'Ame comme indépendante du Corps, puisque sa dépendance n'est que trop bien constatée; ni comme unie à un corps dans un système différent de celui où nous sommes.
>
> [It is not a question of considering Soul as independent of Body, as its dependence is only too well observed; nor as united to a body in a system different from that we are in.][10]

In that perspective, even after rejecting innatism, Condillac was more Cartesian than he thought. No matter how perfect it has become, the power of language remains that of an instrument. Today still, this instrumentalist interpretation of the language/mind duality continues to be alive and powerful in our cultural background. It has become part of a very general instrumentalism I will consider later. For the moment let us confront the phrase "language, instrument of thought."

## *The Systematization of the F-Function*

Going back to my consciousness of the psy-referent, I will say that the downgrading of language to the quality of instrument results from the desire to ascertain the ontological independence of the human mind and its cultural eminence. It supports the common reaction: "language is but language." However, the wish to exalt the purity of our mind and to protect it from language imperfection does not explain why language is understood as instrument and apprehended in its usage. Our former awareness of the pervading presence of the category of instrumentality could suggest an answer: Ceaseless users of language, we cannot help feeling it as a universal operation and in itself an instrumental object. I can stop believing in the independent reality of the psy-referent and continue to say that language is "instrument-of-thought-and-communication." Let us consider the following example. A forerunner in the field of theoretical physics, P. Dirac declared: "Mathematics is the *tool* specially suited for dealing with abstract concepts of any kind."[11] Such a statement is literally true. There is a vast and diversified domain of applied mathematics where mathematical operations and models are used as instruments in any kind of experimentation on abstract concepts, be they logical, physical, psychological, and so on. However, in Dirac's sentence, the word 'tool' implies a vague and metaphorical meaning; also vague is the expression 'dealing with': it is a synonym of 'applying to.' Then we arrive at an endemic problem of modern epistemology: How shall we understand the obvious success of mathematics in their application to natural and social sciences? As many mathematicians would say, the application of a mathematical model is not identical with the construction of that model. Language can be used or become instrumental just because it implies something else. Such is the ambiguity and self-confessed obscurity of the Cartesian position: the "something else" is the psy-referent and its independent, inaccessible universe. Language without the instrumentality of the sign would be pure thinking. Conversely, mind incarnated in body becomes this special instrument called language. Shall we say, language is more than its usage? Are we thus condemned to the hypothesis of the psy-referent? Or, if we are reluctant to use that metaphysical evasion, ***what else is language if it is more than its usage***? That question invites us to face the idea of instrument in its generalization and in the philosophical systematization of the F-function.

Before discussing the historical processing of that systematization, let us be clearly conscious of the strange epistemological situation created by the Cartesian instrumentalization of language, which was at least implicitly accepted for two centuries, even by its apparent opponents. There are two created realities: the world and the mind, the second being the representation of the first and developing its own universe, which will be called 'civilization' or 'culture' as opposed to 'nature.' In its intellectual endeavors human mind is helped by language, the importance of which is more and more recognized. However, language per se is reduced to the role of an epiphenomenon. In its instrumental capacity, it facilitates the actions of the mind, like a wheelchair for a paralytic. It seems to have no reasons for existing except practical ones. It is the humble servant of a prestigious master. Its destiny is to be ignored as soon as it completes its function. It is as transparent as those servants who wait on the brilliant banquets at Court. Condillac's philosophy proposes the best account of the experience of linguistic transparency: Language reaches its best expression and efficiency when, restoring the natural order of things in analytical discourses it realizes such a clear consciousness that words draw aside to give way to ideas. As a perfect servant who plays the role of intermediary between mind and nature, self-effacing language makes itself forgotten. To take account of that situation, Descartes invoked the impenetrable will of God; Condillac, *Genesis* and the dogma of original sin. Aspiring after an invisible state, language is the visible servant of an invisible master who is by himself pure light and mirror. Its images help to recover the lost clarity. But one of those convergent metaphors contributes to explaining not only the historical or even prehistorical appearance of language, but, more importantly, the very essence of instrumentality, all the more so that in order to explain instrumentality, I need an instrument to make an instrument; and to say that intelligence is that sort of instrument does not help very much! One comes back to the old idea of faculty, or its modern form of function, or to an implicit naturalism, a refuge we have already discarded. We can just note that we are reaching the secret and modern *conversion of naturalism into instrumentalism,* that is, what I have already called the philosophical systematization of the F-function.

It has received many names, the most familiar being 'pragmatism,' in reference to the Golden Age of American philosophy, with its exponents, C. S. Peirce, William James, and John Dewey. However, the philosophy of the F-function has taken many forms that are different incarnations of the modern spirit, as announced by Descartes' *Discourse,* when, in its sixth part, he opposes to the speculative philosophy of Scholasticism, a "practical philosophy"

> par laquelle connaissant la force et les actions du feu, de l'eau, de l'air, des astres, des cieux et de tels autres corps qui nous environnent, aussi distinctement que nous connaissons les divers métiers de nos artisans, nous les pourrions employer en même façon à tous les usages auxquels ils sont propres, et ainsi nous rendre comme maîtres et possesseurs de la nature.
>
> [by means of which, knowing the force and action of fire, water, air, the stars, heavens, and all other bodies that environ us, as distinctly as we know the different crafts of our artisans, we can in the same way employ them in all those uses to which they are adapted, and thus render ourselves the masters and possessors of nature.][12]

I regret that the *"comme"* which precedes *"maîtres et possesseurs"* was not rendered in English; truly it is very often forgotten when Descartes is quoted in French: "comme" attenuates the dream of modern anthropocracy; for Descartes man's power is not comparable to God's omnipotence!

The presence of the F-language in Descartes' text is obvious (*'pratique,' 'employer', 'usage', 'rendre comme maîtres et possesseurs'* and the comparison with the craftmanship of the artisans). As historians have justly demonstrated, Descartes was at the same time the defender of the psy-referent through his dualism, and the promoter of a new philosophy of action and of a new language, so that he should be recognized as the Father Founder of these contemporary brothers and adversaries—Marxism and Pragmatism.

## *Marxism and the Concept of Praxis*

The duality between nature and human mind is maintained by Karl Marx. In that line, he is a direct heir of eighteenth-century naturalism; but, with the help of Hegel's philosophy of consciousness and the generalization of dialectical power, he changed this fundamental duality into a practical relation, source of any other kind of relation: the human *praxis* that is exclusive and universal human experience. Nature and mind are not two distinct realities that interact. In themselves they are constituted by their relation, which is not perception nor contemplation, but, on the contrary, that type of action that simultaneously *makes* nature and mind in the very act of manual labor; and thus it transforms reality into a unique mixture of economical and political fabrication, where intellectual life serves as a complex instrumental theory of labor. A new economic model is posited: Being = Praxis = Labor = Culture. As a result, no human being is a given nature with given abilities; he or she is individual-and-collective praxis. In the exercise of that praxis, man *makes* his history, his personality, his values, his social situation. At the same time, he is made by it. That double condition of activity and passivity is projected in the historical relation of master and slave, which governs all societies. There are different levels of praxis and labor. Societies establish hierarchies between them; but, in their varieties, human actions are all conditioned and explicable by the basic and material praxis, original source of infinite, direct, or disguised forms of slavery and freedom.

One can easily understand why Marxist language has exerted such a large and deep influence in our century. It transposes the two opposing languages of realism and idealism into one; it avoids the metaphysical arbitrariness of traditional materialisms and spiritualisms; it transfers the undecipherable antinomy of moral liberty and scientific determinism into the historico-dialectical revolutionary development of mankind. It gives to our linguistic consciousness the satisfactory feeling of a double anchoring in nature and culture, in the external world and the interiority of human societies. By its theory of alienation, it offers plausible answers and promises of cure for the pathological state of contemporary human behaviors, which seem to be boxing us in between the two deliriums of paranoid idealism and schizoidal silence.

One may wonder if the Marxist systematization is not just a "superficial" convenience, a sort of placebo that can only offer temporary solace for a deeply rooted anguish. As an effort of total explanation of mankind and reality, Marxism has theoretical weaknesses which had been exposed by its adversaries; but those critics are not convincing in one sense or another. The opposing theories have their own weaknesses, and both share a complementary difficulty when they face the problem of language.

Let us examine and meditate on what seems to be the *Marxist linguistic deadlock* in that matter: like anything else language is part of human praxis, and its specificity consists in the fabrication of signs that contribute to knowledge, social communication, and all forms of culture. It transforms the exterior world as well as humanity itself into an irreversible and progressive process, although the fight of conservative and revolutionary forces is intensely lived within it. In a true Marxist spirit, Sartre, in his *Critique de la raison dialectique,* demonstrates how the alienating power of words, when meanings are reduced to objects and imitate the inertia of the physical universe, makes of man the slave of his own creations, and how language becomes the dictatorial instrument of the ruling classes.

Those facts are undeniable. Clearly and ironically Sartre shows that the devilish viciousness of language is proper not only to the bourgeoisie but to any dominant class, be it the Communist party itself. Behind his Marxist *rideau de parade,* the coauthor of *On a raison de se révolter* reveals an anarchist and individualist faith that, he hopes, can turn language into an instrument of freedom. Such analyses deal with the effects and the general use of language but not with language in its own creative praxis. In other words Marxism permits denouncing language's erroneous applications, specifically in the economic and political fields. As is well known, it is weaker when it tries to extend its critical rectifications to the domain of biology, for example. However that may be, it has not as yet explained how and why language possesses such a mystifying power. Maybe it could be said that the maleficent effects of language are due to its being understood as instrument and that the language of freedom is language expressed outside the domain of the F-function. It is vague and ambiguous to state that human *praxis* is *cause* of language. One misses the specificity of language as compared to other forms of praxis. The supposedly fundamental economic praxis is immediately language—language of labor, language of capital, language of unions, and so on. There is no brute praxis. At the same time, it is physical transformation, understanding of a world vision and a certain conception of the psy-order. Without claiming to judge Marxism in all its doctrinal aspects, we should at least be aware of its limits when facing the philosophy of language. We also know that its theoretical limitations are obviously due to the excessive confidence it puts in the explanatory power of the F-function under the name of praxis.

One of the most important critics of our era, Mikhail Bakhtin, published in 1929 under the name of one of his students, V. N. Voloshinov, a book entitled *Marxism and Philosophy of Language*. This study deserves our attention. Very justly Bakhtin attacks the Saussurian idealist definition of sign and its opposition between synchrony and diachrony. Bakhtin puts the emphasis on *speech* as having a sociological nature and as function of communication; that is, he stresses sign as dialectical dynamism and enunciation. Furthermore he rejects the objectivist Marxism of Nikolas Marr. In his first chapter he insists on the intimate relation between sign and ideology: "Everything ideological possesses meaning; it represents, depicts, or stands for something lying outside itself. In other words it is a *sign. Without signs, there is no ideology.*"[13] Thus, *"Everything ideological possesses semiotic value"* (p. 9). With great perceptiveness, Bakhtin underlines the function of the word as "semiotic material [e.g., inner speech]" (p. 11), and he recognizes that "the interior world" is one of the basic problems of the philosophy of language. One cannot but agree with him when, concluding a chapter devoted to "verbal interaction," he condemns any form of linguistic objectivism as pure scholarly abstraction that ignores the living realities of language; he also refuses any attempt to explain linguistic evolution by "individualo-psychological" laws (p. 98). I agree with Bakhtin's avoidance of the naturalistic sliding I discussed previously. However, even if he presents the F-function in the best appearance of a dialectical power, he does rally the functionalist systematization, that is, the understanding of language through its functions and its usage. He remains under the Cartesian spell and implies the belief that language is the main instrument within the world of human technological tools. He accepts the F-function and its forms and intentions as immediate limits of understanding and determinacy.

### *Pragmatism and the Concept of Market*

The next process in our meditation should start where Bakhtin stopped, and it should expose the implications of such a position. Before taking that step, let us see if pragmatism was more successful than Marxism in its administration of the F-function and in its explication of language in general. We shall consider the pragmatic organization of language in its general spirit, putting aside its different theories. First, pragmatism is analogous to the Marxist semantic operation assimilating Being to Action and Action to Instrument. It diverges in the interpretation of the nature of the instrument. Whereas Marxism makes of instrumentality the quality of a synthetic power that creates totalities on the basis of internal contradictions, pragmatism sees in the human instrument an *analytical process* thanks to which natural powers are identified and controlled. Syntheses come later and are the consequences of analytical divisions, whereas Marxist thought follows the reverse movement. Then, scientific experimentation—not dialectics—is the model of the F-function and the power behind contemporary technical and liberal societies.

Such an instrumental analytism explains why, unlike Marxism, pragmatism remained firmly rooted in the naturalism of the Enlightment; Nature, in which Man is included, is an immediate given from which any human action starts and to which it returns. The basic system of semantic equivalences we referred to a moment ago, takes up a new form: Nature (as Being-in-action) = Energy = Life = Individual Action = Creativity. Any aspect of human thought is a diversification of engineering, from logic as formal engineering to sociology as political engineering.

Pragmatism is also a more or less avowed *economism,* although very different from Marxist promotion of labor. It remains faithful to Adam Smith's optimist liberalism and makes of marketing the center of human activities: at any level of social functioning, the market is the instrumental situation where all other instruments find their distinction, their final sense and finitude. It goes from production to consumption: a product without a market is nothing; a consumer without a market in which to test his demands is less than Robinson Crusoe in his island. Thus the market with its challenging opportunities confers upon human actions the consecration of success or failure. It is the unique truth space, in other words, the space where individual actions are confronted, experienced. There are idea markets as well as food markets. Ideas or food do not appear prior to market. In the human world, they are more than marketable objects, they belong to the market structure within the intimate relation of production and exchange. The market, at once materialized and idealized, converts nature into humanity, the natural struggle for life into a cultural sophisticated battleground, with the contrasting image of individual creativity and sacrifice. Instrument of liberty, the market is liberty of instrument, liberty won by the promotion of Being into function, by the transfer of natural fatality into the consciousness of natural laws. In an apparent paradox, scientific determinism becomes the true and unique instrument of human freedom.

## *Peirce's Pragmaticism and the Concept of Experimentation*

The best example of pragmatism's theoretization is that of Charles S. Peirce in what he called "pragmaticism"—a term "ugly enough to be safe from kidnappers"—in an effort to distinguish himself from popular or loose forms of pragmatisms. In a well-known article "What Pragmatism is,"[14] Peirce promotes the model of the "experimentalist's mind" and of life in the laboratory. With his logical point of view and contrary to William James's psychological approach, Peirce differentiates sharply between experiment and *experimental phenomena* such as, he says, "Hall's phenomenon," "Michelson's phenomenon," "the chessboard phenomenon." "The experimental phenomenon consists in the fact that, when an experimentalist comes to *act* according to a certain scheme that he has in mind, then something else will happen and shatter the doubt of skeptics, like the celestial fire upon the altar of Elijah" (p. 194). Thus "the rational meaning of every proposition lies in the future." Experimentation, as imagined by Peirce within the frame of his deep realism, does not claim that the *Summum Bonum* is pure action and its consequences; it is the sign of the highest expression of reality under the category of thought. The pragmaticist

> makes [the *Summum Bonum*] to consist in that *process of evolution* [my italics] whereby the existent comes more and more to embody those generals which were just now said to be *destined,* which is what we strive to express in calling them *reasonable*. In its higher stages, evolution takes place more and more largely through self-control, and this gives the pragmaticist a sort of justification for making the rational purport to be general. (p. 199)

Peirce finds the last word of his personal pragmaticism in a kind of practical intellectualism—an echo of Descartes' "practical philosophy"—which is in its turn the crowning of an evolutionary vision. Because for him there is no intellectual action without the direct use of signs, "pragmaticism" kills two birds with one philosophy and offers a theory of language as the superior instrument—an instrument required by any other instrument.

Power of adaptation turned toward the future, language is at the heart of all experimental processes. It is understanding and communication. It founds the "triadic form" or "triune reality," of feeling, volition, and thought in such a way that pragmaticism is closely allied to the Hegelian absolute idealism. In an important letter to Lady Welby (October 12, 1904) Peirce observes that "A *Third* is something that brings a First in relation to a Second. *A sign is a sort of Third*" (my italics).[15] A few lines further, he shows how sign is the true operator of the F-function: "It appears to me that the *essential function* of a sign is to render inefficient relations *efficient*—not to set them into action, but to establish a *habit* or *general rule* whereby they will act on occasion" (my italics).

Peirce's linguistic functionalism and evolutionism is based upon a realism inherited from the medieval theologians: "When we think, then, we ourselves, as we are at the moment, *appear as a sign* [my italics]. Now a sign has, as such, three references: first, it is a sign *to* some thought which interprets it; second, it is a sign *for* some object to which in that thought it is equivalent; third, it is a sign *in* some respect or quality, which brings it into connection with its object."[16] At a strictly descriptive level, there is nothing to say against such a structural and functional analysis of a sign with the help of the three prepositions *'to', 'in,'* and *'for'*. However, if we put together all the above statements, we see that Peirce's functionalism is itself based on the double realism of the external world and of the psy-referent, referring themselves finally to a "third" reality, irreducible to the other two.

One can understand why many linguists and philosophers have had to come back to Peirce in order to find a third way opened between Saussurian intellectualism and Marxist praxism. There is no other philosophy that could offer a better account of the omnipresence of functionality without falling into a trivial and superficial philosophy of action. However, description is not explanation. Peirce's ultimate reference to an evolutionist vision shows that he was unable to stay within the limits of a phenomenological analysis. When he posits the double reality of the world and the mind, we understand why he needs a *third* partner to put them into correspondence in a sort of reversible algorithm: W = F(Psy) and Psy = F(W). Like many others, Peirce was caught within the trap of the double realism of exterior and interior beings, and he converted the Cartesian-confessed obscurity of their union into a universal correspondence. The mystery of language remains in full, even after he has realized the universality of the correspondence function.

Let us return to the text defining the triple semiotic to-, in-, and for-function. The introductory phrasing is revealing: "Now a sign, as such *has three references*" (my italics). The use of the verb 'to have' suggests that Peirce was not ready to give up the priority of Being over function and to write "a sign is." Furthermore, he implies that the triadic function of the sign relies on its referential power; but the rest of the text shows that for him, a reference implies the preliminary referents of the world and the human mind. Then, we find ourselves in a confused, even if currently accepted, situation: the function of 'function' is to establish three simultaneous references, and the general function of reference is to make possible these three references. It is a cat-and-mouse game between reference and function, both distinct and the same. We shall understand how and why a reference becomes a function, or, in Peircean terms, how and why one can establish a habit or a general rule. What is a habit? What is a rule? Peirce tries to avoid William James's psychologism. Has he really succeeded in his effort? Or does he succeed in just making of 'habit' and 'rule' two indefinable substitutes to 'sign' and finally, to 'function'? Again and again, the same question reappears: Do we have to comply with the three prerequisites of the world, the mind and the function, in order to confer on our linguistic ability the condition without which it could not be used and which can be understood either as a metaphysical evidence or as a logical a priori or as a psychosociological convenience? The present question itself contains a vicious circle: it presupposes what is at stake, the very emergence of the word 'function' and its indefinite lexical field.

Two philosophers looked for an answer to this very difficult problem: "How is the F-function understood in its instrumental process?" Or, said more simply, "What is an instrument and what is its function?" Henri Bergson and Martin Heidegger, each in his personal style proposed European versions of pragmatism and probably reached the deepest interpretations of the modernist transfer of Being into Action. We are still more or less, consciously or not, depending on their language for our open or hidden epistemologies. Thus we will meditate on these languages, not from the point of view of historians of ideas and philosophies, who implicitly believe in the existence of the psy-referent, but being aware of a semantic and existential mutation in the historical universe of our language.

## *Bergson and the Functionality of Human Intelligence*

Let us begin with a full bath of Bergsonian language, starting with the famous definitions of intelligence and intuition in *L'Evolution créatrice:*

> *l'intelligence, envisagée dans ce qui paraît être sa démarche originelle, est la faculté de fabriquer des objets artificiels, en particulier des outils à faire des outils, et d'en varier indéfiniment la fabrication.* (Bergson's italics)
>
> [intelligence, considered in what seems to be its original feature [*démarche*] is the faculty of manufacturing [*fabriquer*] artificial objects, especially tools to make tools, and of indefinitely varying the manufacture.][17]

Then, at the end of the next paragraph, appears this remark: "l'instinct achevé est une faculté d'utiliser et même de construire des instruments organisés; l'intelligence achevée est la faculté de fabriquer et d'employer des instruments inorganisés" ("instinct perfected is a faculty of using and even constructing organized instruments; perfected intelligence is the faculty of making [*fabriquer*] and using unorganized instruments."[18] Later the key word '*fabriquer*' is defined this way: "*Fabriquer consiste à former la matière, à l'assouplir et à la plier, à la convertir en instrument, afin de s'en rendre maître*" (p. 650) [Fabricating consists in shaping matter, in making it supple and in bending it, in converting it into an instrument in order to become master of it] (p. 201). Life, as action, is fabrication, that is, *transformation of matter into form.* There are two kinds of forms—living organisms and static instruments or mechanisms, with a specific differentiation: "*Le signe instinctif est un signe* adhérent, *le signe intelligent est un signe* mobile" (p. 629) [The instinctive sign is adherent, the intellect sign is mobile] (p. 175). In functional terms, Bergson adds the following comment:

> La vie, non contente de produire des organismes, voudrait leur donner comme appendice la matière inorganisée elle-même, convertie en un immense organe par l'industrie de l'être vivant." (p. 632)
>
> [Life, not content with producing organisms, would like to give them as an appendage inorganic matter itself, converted into an immense organ by the industry of the living being.] (p. 178)

If I follow correctly the Bergsonian lexical arabesque of semantic correspondence, intelligence transforms matter into inert instrument, here called *"organe"* (with an implicit reference to the Aristotelian *organon*), and adds it to the living organisms in order to improve its power of action. Thus the words 'form' and 'instrument' constitute a semantic circle. Both are means of action and functions because by itself a form is a relation "entre la situation donnée et les moyens de l'utiliser" (p. 623) [between a given situation and the means of utilizing it] (p. 166). When intelligence develops its fabrication of an instrument, its knowledge is essentially formal; "il porte sur des rapports" (p. 623) [it bears on relations] (p. 166) and demonstrates a considerable advantage over the *material* knowledge of instinct. "Une forme, justement parce qu'elle est vide, peut être remplie tour à tour, à volonté, par un nombre indéfini de choses, même par celles qui ne servent à rien" (p. 623) [A form, just because it is empty, may be filled at will with any number of things, even with those that are not of use] (p. 166).

At the center of the human universe of forms-instruments, *language appears to be the ideal instrument for making instruments:*

> Mais l'homme n'entretient pas seulement sa machine, il arrive à s'en servir comme il lui plaît. Il le doit sans doute à la supériorité de son cerveau . . . Il le doit à son langage, qui fournit à la conscience un corps immatériel où s'incarner et la dispense ainsi de se poser exclusivement sur les corps matériels dont le flux l'entraînerait d'abord, l'engloutirait bientôt. Il le doit à la vie sociale . . . Mais notre cerveau, notre société et notre langage ne sont que les signes extérieurs et divers d'une seule et même supériorité interne. (pp. 719–20)
>
> [But man not only maintains his machine, he succeeds in using it as he pleases. Doubtless he owes it to the superiority of his brain . . . . He owes it to his language, which furnishes consciousness with an immaterial body in which to incarnate itself and thus exempts it from dwelling exclusively on material bodies, whose flux would soon drag it along and finally swallow it up. He owes it to social life . . . . But our brain, our society, and our language are only the external and various signs of one and the same internal superiority.] (pp. 288–89)

What have signs in common? The power of "informing" matter, of giving form to it. One will note the oxymoron "immaterial body," suggested by a striking conspiracy between the psy-referent and the F-function.

Aiming at the destruction of the two great formalisms of Aristotle and

Kant, Bergson's meditation secretly centers itself around the idea of form and fabrication of forms. In the last chapter of *L'Evolution créatrice,* dominated by the cinematographical example, a section is entitled "Form and Becoming." There one finds a new definition of form: *"la forme n'est qu'un instantané pris sur une transition"* [*form is only a snapshot view of a transition*] (p. 328). Knowledge possesses a cinematographical character:

> La méthode cinématographique est donc la seule pratique, puisqu'elle consiste à régler l'allure générale de la connaissance sur celle de l'action, en attendant que le détail de chaque acte se règle à son tour sur celui de la connaissance. (p. 754)
>
> [The cinematographical method is therefore the only practical method since it consists in making the general character of knowledge form itself on that of action, while expecting that the detail of each act depends in its turn on that of knowledge.] (p. 333)

Indeed, Bergson condemns the traditional philosophy of Ideas, which from Artistotle to Kant results from the application of the "cinematographical method" of the intellect to the experience of what he calls "creative evolution" or "spiritual energy." Doing so, he passes from the relative opposition between instinct and intelligence, between two kinds of instrumentalization, to the absolute opposition between intuition and intelligence, that is, between the action with instrument and the action freed from the technique that suspends the vital impetus and formalizes it. To try to define intuition would be to put oneself into a patent contradiction and to reduce it to a conceptual form. In itself, it is ineffable, beyond the limits and abilities of the language instrument. It is pure spiritual energy. Thus, at that level of philosophical consciousness, Bergson rediscovers and reinterprets Cartesian dualism: he asserts the independent reality of the psyreferent; but, contrary to Descartes, it is an inaccessible referent because our present life is that of our body and our brain. Nevertheless, we can *use* the word 'intuition' in negative and even in positive ways:

> l'intuition pourra nous faire saisir ce que les données de l'intelligence ont d'insuffisant et nous laisser entrevoir les moyens de les compléter. D'un côté, en effet, elle utilisera le mécanisme même de l'intelligence, à montrer comment les cadres intellectuels ne trouvent plus ici leur exacte application, et, d'autre part, par son travail propre, elle nous suggérera tout au moins le sentiment vague de ce qu'il faut mettre à la place des cadres intellectuels. (pp. 645–46)

> [intuition enables us to grasp what it is that intelligence fails to give us, and indicates the means of supplementing it. On the one hand, it will utilize the mechanisms of intelligence itself to show how intellectual molds cease to be strictly applicable; and on the other hand, by its own work, it will suggest to us the vague feeling, if nothing more, of what must take place of intellectual molds.] (p. 195)

In other words, intuition invites language to surpass itself, to act against its own function, to become instrument correcting instruments on behalf of a reality that is at the same time present and absent, life itself, as creative and paradoxical power of instrumental forms that change life itself into informed matter, and Time (*durée*) into space.

How is this possible? Here is Bergson's answer: By bringing back the form of concept instrument in contact with the form at its least instrumental and functional quality, the *image*. Then, the language of the F-function, which cannot be surpassed, as the quotations above amply prove, ceases to be purely functional. Poetry offers the best example of the presence/absence of intuition within language; it is language sacrificing itself for its absolute Referent:

> L'idée génératrice d'un poème se développe en des milliers d'imaginations, lesquelles se matérialisent en phrases qui se déploient en mots. Et, plus on descend de l'idée immobile, enroulée sur elle-même, aux mots qui la déroulent, plus il y a de place laissée à la contingence et au choix, d'autres métaphores, exprimées par d'autres mots, eussent pu surgir; une image a été appelée par une image, un mot par un mot. Tous ces mots courent maintenant les uns derrière les autres, cherchant en vain, par eux-mêmes, à rendre la simplicité de l'idée génératrice. Notre oreille n'entend que les mots; elle ne perçoit donc que des accidents. Mais notre esprit, par bonds successifs, *saute des mots aux images* [my italics],des images à l'idée originelle, et remonte ainsi, de la perception des mots, accidents provoqués par des accidents, à la conception de l'Idée qui se pose elle-même. Ainsi procède le philosophe en face de l'univers. (pp. 765–66)

> [The generative idea of a poem is developed in thousands of imaginations which are materialized in phrases that spread themselves out in words. And the more we descend from the motionless idea, wound on itself, to the words that unwind it, the more room is left for contingency and choice. Other metaphors, expressed by other words, might have arisen; and image is called up by an image, a word by a word. All these words run now one after another, seeking in vain, by themselves, to give back the simplicity of the generative idea. Our ear only hears the words; it therefore

> perceives only accidents. But our mind, by successive *leaps ["bonds"] from the words to the images* (my italics), from the image to the original idea, and so gets back, from the perception of words—accidents called up by accidents—to the conception of the Idea that posits its being. So the philosopher proceeds, confronted with the universe.] (p. 348)

The word 'Idea,' capitalized, refers directly to Schopenhauer's *Aesthetics*. It suggests that poetry and philosophy, insofar as they follow the poetic model, are languages of action at the minimum of their functional intention; they are contemplative experience. Within them words lose their conceptual structure; they are converted into images. Language is freed from the deterministic codes that govern its logic and grammar; it has become inspired language of images, even if the surface we perceive is covered by a solid paving of words.

To give to the word 'image' its full Bergsonian impact we have to go back from the language of *L'Evolution créatrice* to that of *Matière et mémoire:* our thought is only a sketch of the body in the conditional sense. The images of our representation

> ne sont pas représentées à la conscience sans que se dessinent à l'état d'esquisse ou de tendance, les mouvements par lesquels ces images *se joueraient* elles-mêmes dans l'espace—je veux dire imprimeraient au corps telles ou telles attitudes—dégageraient tout ce qu'elles contiennent implicitement de mouvement spatial (p. 165)
>
> [are not represented to consciousness without movements outlining themselves in one form of sketches or trends, by these movements those images *would play themselves* in space—I mean to say they would impart to the body such and such attitudes, and release all that implicit spatial movement they contain] (my translation)

Confronting psychology and metaphysics, Bergson assigns to both the same object of study: the human mind; but psychology considers its functioning in practical life, whereas metaphysics strives to liberate it from the condition of practical action (*l'action utile*) and to recapture it as pure creative energy (pp. 167/169).

I apologize for quoting Bergson so extensively. I wished to restore in its full complexity and brilliance Bergson's writing building up its referential power. In our century I do not know of a better evidence. Thus, we have reached the deepest implications and motivations of the Bergsonian endeavor to formulate the language of action thanks to the interpenetration of two languages within the F-function experienced on the double plane of physical and metaphysical realities, that is, of body and mind. When Bergson gives to psychology and metaphysics their respective "functions," he designates metaphysics as the *disinterested* translation of utilitarian psy-language, with the transfer of *form instrument* into *image form*. Doing so, in spite of contrary statements, and like his predecessors in the Western world, he remains captive of the myth of the Fall, older than the Platonic-Christian vision (the Fall of the Soul into the prison of the body). Language partakes of that ontological corruption; it needs to be purified. As such, it has no direct access to the world of the Pure Spirit; but it makes possible the correction of human experience and its return to its original state. The actual return will wait however until death permits the separation of mind and body or better, until life conquers death. In the meanwhile, intuition will serve as the stimulating and instrumental cause of Metaphysics—language against language, language partially freed not from its bodily rooting, but from its bodily functions. Read in that perspective, Bergsonian metaphysics is much more than its transparent message. This dual philosophy of action and the F-function hide a philosophy of language that is pure linguistic action and, in its etymological sense, true re-formation. Thus, language is no longer condemned to the marginal, representative function that Descartes attributes to it. It is the center and present aim of evolution, even if on the surface the vision function seems predominant. If we take seriously that secret Bergsonian teaching, we cannot help feeling that we should try to dis-implicate this deep linguistic intelligence, not only from the mythology of the Fall, but more importantly from the realist and idealist postulates from which Bergson never succeeded in disentangling himself in spite of his deliberate attempt to do so.

Bergson did not realize that denouncing the linguistic and theoretical weakness of modern realisms and idealisms was not enough, especially to being liberated from the psy-referent. Even when he unveils the static vision behind the Greek philosophy of Ideas, he continues to understand language as the instrument of the mind. Here lies the *coup de force* thanks to which realism and idealism join forces in the belief in the independence of the psy-referent.

To sum up, Bergson's meditation on the relation of action and language and his endeavor to interpret language behavior with the help of the language of the F-function were ineffectual. To say that language is action and category of action helps to explain the effects of language in the varied practical fields of which human cultures are composed, but that does not take into account the so-called essence of language, which founds the hows and whys; and it does not consider the converse proposition: "if language *is* action, in the accepted sense that it serves action, the always forgotten inversion deserves our heed: action *is* language, in the sense that it serves language." Let us be reminded again of Pascal's warning: a primitive concept cannot be used to define another primitive concept; action cannot explain language, and language be reduced to action. Furthermore, Bergson took for granted the internal connection within the F-function between the concepts of action, function, utility, instrument, and so on. Surprisingly enough, nowhere, not even in *L'Evolution créatrice,* is there a description of the concept of instrument nor a discussion about the disputable differentiation between instinctive and intellectual instruments, except in a very general way. Likewise, the concept of use is accepted as an obvious quality of action. It is then difficult to understand the basic meaning of a "disinterested" act or the paradox of "use without use."

## *Heidegger's Readiness-to-Hand*

Indeed, I could have reached those conclusions without insisting on the detailed exposition of the Bergsonian philosophy of intuition. I did it, first in a special effort to replay, so to speak, some revealing phases of this great metaphysical adventure, and second, because its own theoretical expression permeated the problematics of all philosophies afterward: it was one of the two most innovative imaginings of our modernist linguistic experience. Now we shall turn to Martin Heidegger, who is the obvious second model of contemporary innovations in the philosophical language put at our disposal. His work on German language went further and deeper than Hegel and Husserl's own writing imaginations: and, contrary to Bergson, he directly explored the obscure genesis of the F-function in its instrumentality and utility. We already discussed Heidegger's existential realism, his description of the *Dasein* as double "praesens" of understanding-of-being and being-of-understanding, thus as a paradoxical prelinguistic experience of language: "The doctrine of signification is rooted in the ontology of *Dasein.*"[19] At this moment, in our meditation on the F-function and its powerful lexicon, we are able to complete this statement: the *Dasein,* not words, is source of meaning and discourse, because in itself it has the quality of "disclosuredness," "uncoveredness," linked to *functionality.* Being-in-the-world, this basic determination of *Dasein*'s existence, is "the presupposition for being able to apprehend anything at all."[20] One page later, involving himself and us in the "praesens" of his writing, Heidegger exposes the intimate relation of sense and function: "We always already understand the world in holding ourselves in a *contexture of functionality,* i.e., the contexture of significance (*Bedeutsamkeit*)."[21] Without exaggerating we could say that *Being and Time* in its entirety is the philosophical experiment of the functional power of the *Dasein,* that is, a direct experience of instrumentality or, better, of "instrumenthood." That means direct *involvement* and *serviceability:*

> With this thing, for instance, which is ready-to-hand, and which we accordingly call a "hammer," there is an involvement in hammering. . . . In a workshop, for example, the totality of involvement which is constitutive for the ready-to-hand in its readiness to hand, is 'earlier' than any single item of equipment; so too for the farmstead with all its utensils and outlying lands.[22]

Consequently, the notions of involvement, serviceability, and equipment are primordial experiences of the *Dasein;* they precede the universe of human tools (signs included) and a fortiori the universe of objects as seen by traditional ontologies.

Let us meditate on the following text that may help us understand how the notion of function is subjacent to that of being:

> The Greek had an appropriate term for 'things': *prágmata*—that is to say, that which one has to do in one's concernful dealings (*praxis*). But ontologically, the specifically 'pragmatic' character of the *prágmata* is just what the Greek left in obscurity; they thought of these 'proximally' as 'mere Things.' We shall call those entities which we encounter in concern "equipment." In our dealings we come across equipment for writing, sewing, working, transportation, measurement. The kind of Being which equipment possesses must be exhibited. The clue for doing this lies in our first defining what makes an item of equipment—namely, its equipmentality. (pp. 96–97)

Heidegger proposes this "defining":

> The kind of Being which equipment posseses—in which it manifests itself in its own right—we call "readiness-to-hand" [*Zuhandenheit*]. "The hammering does not simply have knowledge about [*um*] the hammer's character as equipment, but it has appropriated this equipment in a way which

> could not be more suitable. . . . The hammering itself uncovers the specific 'manipulability' [*Handlichkeit*] of the hammer." Equipment belongs to the world of the "in-order-to" and the "towards-which." It is intimate function of the *Dasein* as care (*Sorge*): The Being of the *Dasein* means ahead-of-itself-Being-already-in (the-world) as Being alsongside (entities encountered within the world). (p. 237)

In conclusion, "Because Being-in-the world is eventually care, Being-alongside the ready-to-hand could be taken in our previous analyses as concern" (p. 237).

Although those quotations are only a small part of Heidegger's enterprise in recapturing and interpreting the F-function immanent in German language, they should be sufficient to underline the originality of such a labor of writing in order to fight linguistic transparency in the universal perspective of functionality. Through the experience of the *Dasein* in its preontological understanding, we can ourselves understand how and why the F-function surrounds and interprets the world of objects and subjects and its multiple languages. If one translates Heidegger's descriptions into common language, one could say that in our respective experiences, our mind and our world are closely related within the concern and care of the readiness-to-hand. In a philosophical way, Heidegger gives to the classical categories of causality and finality an existential, preontological meaning.

We are far from Descartes indeed! It is as if Heidegger were shedding some light on "the obscure union of mind and body" and rooting innate clear ideas in a primordial obscure acting-understanding. However, the philosopher of *Being and Time* stays Cartesian when he subordinates all his demonstrations to the existential postulate of the psy-referent. His writings, as descriptions and demonstrations, concern the *Dasein* as *independent referent*. In a manner similar to many pragmatists, or more generally, to all the philosophers of our century, he constantly sends back his own language to a reality in front of which language forgets itself, even effaces itself. Heidegger reproaches Hobbes and nominalism in general with finally *surrendering* to the "whatness" of the thing about which an assertion is made; but he himself *surrenders* to the "whoness" of the *Dasein*. In spite of repeated denegations, his writings are comparable to floating veils that help to understand and see the Being of the *Dasein*. Unveiling the veils put around Being and Time by traditional ontology, he replaces them by what he hopes are transparent veils, but he does not prove that his writing is by itself radical uncoveredness of the psy-referent.

The mystery of language remains intact. It is too easy a solution to see in it an important part of the ready-to-hand, and to define a sign as "an item of equipment which explicitly raises a totality of equipment into our circumspection so that together with it the worldy character of the ready-to-hand announces itself" (p. 110). Nothing is said about the key problems without which there can be no satisfactory philosophy of language: (1) *if language is part of our equipment, what is its relation with the other parts*? Needless to say, our technological civilization has opted for dreadful solutions! (2) *What is the relation between the understanding of Being and the understanding of language,* or, reciprocally, what sort of circle is there between the understanding of language and the language of understanding? Not without haste Heidegger has justified the hermeneutic circle! I am afraid it hides an authentic vicious circle that consists in implying the preliminary existence of Being to explain language and in implying the existence of language to explain Being. Another aspect of this circle is the relation between things and functions, entity and functionality, being and acting.

The conclusion to our meditation on the F-function and its philosophical systematizations called "pragmatism" is both disappointing and frustrating. Pragmatism, even in the subtlest forms of philosophies of intuition or *Dasein,* did not succeed in surpassing or avoiding the postulates of realism and of the psy-referent. Beliefs in a being independent of language or in a mind that is a subject and object of language subsist in open or disguised ways, although all those philosophies agree on the idea that the realist-idealist antinomy is artificial and should be discarded. When Heidegger declares that "the hammering itself uncovers the specific 'manipulability' of the hammer," is he not returning to the too famous "dormitive virtue" of opium in a modern variant of essentialism as functional innatism? Is this not the risk run by the phenomenological method when it offers a description with the secret hope of conferring upon it the power of a demonstration?

## *The Semantic Irradiation of the F-Function*

Whatever the theoretical weaknesses of pragmatism in all its aspects may be, we cannot condemn it and its implications without recognizing its raison d'être. It is not by accident that the F-function possesses such a universal capacity of semantic irradiation. Its association with the realist principle of independent Being and with the postulate of the psy-referent can continue to play a decisive role even when their ontological implications are suspended. I may say, "if, for whatever reason, I believe in the existence of an independent referent, I cannot speak or write about it without the intervention of the F-function," or, "if I refer to our mind as independent psychological realities, then I cannot help considering them as cluster of functions." Those "ifs" are understood as imaginary suppositions, analogous to the suppositions that initiate a mathematical demonstration and disappear at the moment of the Q.E.D. In other words, the F-function does not require the help of the realist principle or the psy-referent postulate in order to organize our languages. It was the correct intuition of the pragmatic trend in our modern cultures; it failed only when those cultures were unable to experience language outside of its instrumental condition.

Let us consider the status of the statement, "language is a function of the human mind," once it has been purified of its realist, idealist, spiritualist implications. It means that I recognize language as one of the abilities (ability being one of the numerous possible synonyms of function) of our minds, such as the ability to speak and write. It is as if I were writing: "language is language, that is, a linguistic function." Obviously I prefer to write, "language is function," because I feel that the word 'function' should help me escape pure redundancy. In what way? What is a linguistic function? This question has a neat ontological character I can feign to forget, but I cannot feign knowing that in my language 'function' has multiple applications with which the linguistic function should be compared, such as the mathematical, physical, chemical, biological, psychological, sociological. Now, I am no longer speaking of a specific ability to behave, but of a certain property of being and of behaving in a regional field. Then I can say that the linguistic function (I shall call it $F_1$) is formalized by modern scientific logics and that its laws are looked for in psychology or sociology. I can also decide that $F_1$ is irreducible to any other function and imagine an independent science called 'linguistics.' Whatever my decision will be, it will add nothing to my initial statement concerning the identification of language and function. Furthermore, well-known insoluble epistemological problems come crowding in, such as the relation of logical and mathematical functions, the differentiation of biology and sociology, physical reductionism, hierarchism Popper style, and so on.

Let us make another try. 'Function' is a word in our dictionaries, a word among many others; so let us invoke a principle of linguistic sufficient reason but corrected by what I earlier called linguistic contingency and wisdom: what is function of 'function' in our lexical corpus? Why did such a word exist? Or in a similar manner, why did it appear in any known language (or its equivalents)? These questions seem to belong to genetic and comparative linguistics but are loaded with philosophical implications, as studies like Benveniste's *Indo-European Language and Society* (*Le Vocabulaire des institutions indo-européennes*) amply demonstrate. As far as I know, the most original endeavor in that perspective was made by Heidegger and his meditations on the "facticity" of the *Dasein,* but we have seen that those deep and brilliant analyses come down to writing "function is function," and the passage of the experience of functionality to the word 'function' remains a mystery. Nevertheless Heidegger deserves our recognition for his insistence on the fact that the Being-of-the-There (*Da-sein*) *is* its immediate understanding. One may even wonder why Heidegger did write 'understanding' instead of 'language,' if not under the pressure of his belief in a psy-referent.

## *Prerequisites of the Mathematical Function*

If we follow this trend of thought, we can posit that "there is no existence without its language." I may say that the relation of being and language makes of language the function of being and that that function is called "understanding." From there I can pass to the idea that function is the universal qualification of being-*as*-understood. I could even condense the last phrase and state that "being-as" indicates the linguistic function of understanding. Finally, why not say that 'as'—that particle I cannot avoid and that reappears constantly in my own writing—is the *universal functional index.* "As" would be the source of the operations as they are formalized in the calculus of propositional functions. Let us look at the first pages of an introduction to mathematic analysis, devoted to the pair "set-function."[23] After a brief, intuitive presentation of the word 'set' and its operational postulates, comes the first definition: "A function is a non-empty set X, a non-empty set Y, and a rule of correspondence *f* which associates with each element *x* X a unique element *y* Y." This definition is immediately followed by two nominal conventions: "The element *y* associated with a given element *x* X is denoted *f(x)* and we write $y = f(x)$; *y* is called *the image* of *x* under *f,* and *x* is called a *preimage* of *y*" (pp. 2–3).

My present problem concerns neither the philosophy of mathematics nor mathematical analysis itself but more simply, what appears today to be the basic definition in mathematical analysis under the name of function. It requires the concept of *set* as mathematical being, the *given* existence of two non-empty sets and the association of two sets thanks to the so-called rule of correspondence between the elements of the two sets in a one-to-one (univoque) correspondence. Thus, once this precondition is given (two distinct non-empty sets), function is characterized by three words: 'association,' 'correspondence,' and 'rule.' The first two are synonymous; an association, at its highest generality, is act or state of correspondence, but in a peculiar way: one term of the correspondence is the *image* of another term (*preimage*). That correspondence is realized by the application of a *rule* making the element of one set the image of the other. Needless to say, the word 'image' here has no psychological import; it is a conventional decision, a nominal definition: "image of . . ." designates simultaneously a state of correspondence or association and an act resulting from the application of a rule. Indeed, the mathematical vocabulary, especially in its first steps, cannot be pure denotation without connotation. For those of us who do not pretend to interpret the development of mathematical analysis but, more modestly, who mean to recapture the contingent necessity of the word 'function', we can conclude that, in the case of mathematical language, 'function' is put into mathematical existence with the double precondition of a being as *set of elements* and a given duality $(x, y)$; then it is qualified as rule *and* image.

Shall we say that 'rule' and 'image' specify 'being as . . .'? Yes, insofar as 'being as . . .' suggests a limitation of being, that is, a being subordinated to certain conditions of existence. A lexico-analysis of 'as' shows that this conjunction falls under the categories of "motive, supposition, circumstance, event, chance," and all of them have something in common—*subservience:* they mark a dependence. We have already noticed that 'function' is in a similar situation, so that to meditate on "being as . . ." is the same as trying to understand the emergence and the status of 'function' in our vocabulary, whatever it may be, common, philosophical, or scientific. To take the example of mathematics, that emergence is primordial as a textbook puts 'function' as the first word to be defined and, as such, as the source of all possible definitions and demonstrations; it is the condition of mathematical language with the double power of ruling and imaging. There is no understanding of subservience (subordinating $y$ to $x$, movement to acceleration, attraction to distance, respiration to oxygen, production to consumption, love to jealousy, or the reverse, etc.) without the awareness of a rule fixing the mode of subservience and of a being becoming the "image" (in the sense of dependency) of another being.

Here comes the critical problem: how is it possible? How can we pass from 'being' to 'being as . . .'? Or in mathematical phrasing, how can we pass from the concept of set to that of function? The language of the textbook I am consulting—and its lexical situation would be similar for any other textbook—clearly proves that it is impossible to derive 'function' from 'set,' the idea of "dependent correspondence" from that of "a *well-defined* collection of objects called elements." It is obvious that the set will be "well defined" after the position of the definition of the function. If we consider the ideas of collection and element, it is also impossible to derive from them the idea of function. Far from it! On the contrary, one may wonder if the set, specified as relation between collection and element, does not imply, however vaguely, the presence of a functional power. If I think about the set of the twelve months of the year or the set of the twelve tribes of Israel, I can imagine a pure plurality of objects grouped under an arithmetic rule. I can make the effort of thinking those "objects" or "beings" without specifying the number of elements and grasp the set and its elements at a prearithmetic level of perception. After all, birds do that when they are able to differentiate cards with different number of dots! The awareness of sets and elements of sets is thus purified from any functional insinuation. Mathematicians deal with that situation by recognizing the impossibility of a total formalization of their language. As the textbook I am using states from the beginning: "Every language has certain words which are basic and remain undefined but of whose meaning there is universal acceptance" (p. 1). Alas! philosophers have no right to behave in the same manner. It is their very personal duty to meditate on those primordial implications and dependence or subverviences—to meditate on not only the particular case of the relation between set and function but mainly the universalized case of relation of being and function. Such a kind of meditation should be conducted at the two levels of conceptual analysis and of experience.

In classical ontology any being is qualified by its existence and essence. It is obvious that the idea of function cannot be derived from that of existence, unless we admit by a vicious circle that only function exists; and that hypothesis would not tell us what function is. Thus, the real problem lies in the possible relation of function and essence. To get us involved in a fight against pre-Cartesian ontology and its Scholastic language would be useless. It will be enough to observe that the concept of faculty is assimilated to that of the properties of the essence of a certain being, and that there is therefore a permanent confusion between function and essence:

'function' is present in the consciousness of being as soon as the idea of form is understood as the power of informing matter—for instance, of giving to an unspecified matter the form of a collection of elements. In a word, neither Platonism nor Aristotelism nor Thomism can help us in solving our present problem. I apologize for putting aside so lightly very important philosophies, but in the present case, their conceptual situation is simple: beginning with the concept of Being, they are unable to explain the emergence of function, except by adding it without explanation. Function cannot be derived from Being, in the perspective of a philosophy claiming to discover everything from the total comprehensive power of the concept of Being.

Is the situation any better with post-Cartesian ontologies, ontologies that admit the basic existence of one or two realities called matter and mind? As founder of modern analytic geometry Descartes applied the idea of function—which is for him true mathematical *order*—to matter understood as space, number and form, and thus reconciled in one discipline arithmetic and geometry. The idea of space as functional order is innate. The problem of correspondence between that idea and real space or matter is solved by God as guarantor, especially because of his very essence. He cannot be a devilish liar. Descartes' successors, like Malebranche and his vision of a Divine understanding, Spinoza with his theory of infinite and parallel attributes of God, Leibniz with his dream of Preestablished Harmony, even Newton calling for a *Sensorium Dei,* did not succeed in getting out of the theological refuge. For us, those ambitious metaphysical constructions come back to the simple statement that the understanding of space as matter implies the idea of function, so that I cannot understand space without seeing in it a system of functional order, implying a rule and an image. The idea of function remains a free gift of God, as Descartes put it bluntly. As such, it is a property, if not *the* universal property of our mind. Thus our initial problem is finally reduced to the enunciation, *"How can the idea of function be derived from the human mind experiencing itself?"* Again we are back to the psy-referent and its universally recognized "faculties" of Will and Understanding.

First, is the reflective experience of will able to generate the awareness of function? Let us consider the "will to believe." In contemporary philosophies, "belief" in itself remains as mysterious as it was at the time of Hume and Kant. If, after Baudelaire and many others with him, I write that I believe that the world is made of correspondences, underlining the universality of the F-function, there is a gap between my belief in correspondence and my idea of correspondence. In this case, the power of linguistic decision and more generally the power to decide to act cannot be mistaken for the content or form of the decision. I can claim that in its consequence an act has a functional significance and there is no action without initial relation in a world of relations. I can even say that my consciousness of will, especially that of my will to believe, is itself released and sets itself in motion thanks to my "intent" to believe or to initiate such and such action; but I shall have made no progress in generating the idea of function. For more than a century, philosophers have found it convenient to speak of the psy-referent in terms of intentionality. Even if that assimilation had some remarkable and fruitful consequences, as demonstrated by Husserl and his followers, it has failed to prove that intentionality leads to functionality, as we have noted in the case of Heideggerian endeavor: readiness-to-hand is something else than intent-to-be. I can turn and press the ideas of will, acting, intending, as much as I can, I will never extract the idea of function, no more than a wine press full of grapes will produce a drop of orange juice!

I arrive at the last refuge: the essence of the psy-referent is understanding, and understanding is the awareness of functionality. That solution is currently accepted by psychologists. Intelligence—a frequent synonym for understanding—is awareness of relation. Any idea of relation—be it logical, chemical, biological, sociological, and so on—implies that of function. In other words, the experience of understanding is the awareness of the function of being, and the consciousness of understanding—for example, when de Gaulle said to the French Army in Algeria "I have understood you!" or when I mumble "*Je me comprends*" (literally "I understand myself," meaning "I know what I mean"), or when my distinguished colleagues tell me, "We do not understand your way of thinking and your purpose"—when it is expressed, refers to its own understanding as instrumentality of understanding. A gift of God or a gift of nature, my understanding sees itself as a function—function of adaptation, function of organization, function of remembrance, and so on. What does it prove? Simply that I cannot understand understanding or anything else without the help of the idea of function, so that understanding *is* the experience of functionality, or function thinking. The mystery remains intact even if I compare it to the clarity of light! Nevertheless when I speak of the clarity of my mind, I suggest more than the assimilation of understanding to function, I make of 'function' a universal property of my mind.

Then comes the question, "*How is my mind as mind, function?*" Such a question calls for another, "*What is mind as mind?*" As is well known and largely demonstrated by Bergson, only a mind "knows" what mind is. If one tries to say more, one will enter the subtle domain of understanding by negation and even by reciprocal negation: mind is the opposite of matter . . . and matter the opposite of mind. We have already been conscious of the difficulty raised by the belief in the independent existence of a psy-referent, and it should be enough to make us skeptical about the chance of deriving function from mind. Furthermore, at this new point of meditation, there is something more significant: if matter is contrary to mind, how is it possible that material space has become in modern sciences the ideal domain of functional applications and thus, that mind has become the locus of the true understanding of the physical world? That question leads to the empirist, idealist, and pragmatic solutions, which, their differences put aside, have something in common: ***human mind is experience,*** either with the help of innate or a priori forms or as empty form waiting to be filled.

### *Exposing the Word 'Experience'*

Have we finally caught the culprit responsible for our difficulties, well hidden behind the theoretical parades of philosophers—the word 'experience,' which in modern thinking took under its cover and practice the obscure union of mind and body? That union has become the relation between the *experiencer* (the mind) and the *experienced* (the matter), both meeting on the ground of *experience*. Experience would be the battlefield of the F-function, usually and conveniently framed by the hypothetical psy- or matter-referents. But I have learned to be suspicious of those conveniences, and I have found no satisfactory proof of the existence of such referents posited as realities independent of our language. As a philosopher I should even learn to live my experience of writing without them.

Let us confront 'function' and 'experience.' Is any semantic derivation or communication possible between them? First, what does it mean to say with Peirce that human action at its highest expression is experimental? Surely it is a commendable effort to overcome the common post-Cartesian dualism of mind and matter and to avoid the two classical explanations: experience is passive reception of an external, physical action thanks to our sensory organs—reception that changes itself into a psychological activity made of associations and habits re-presenting and re-living in their own reflective manner the varieties of the physical universe; or else experience is an active transformation and elaboration of a passive, sensorial reception, thanks to the application of intellectual forms to the given sensorial. Today nobody would accept either one of these models, although they remain vaguely present in our epistemological background. Studies like Ian Hacking's *Representating and Intervening* clearly show how difficult it is, if not impossible, to escape dualism even when experience is considered as a primordial property of human mind and when the theory of sensory data is rejected.

Then, what we noted about 'function' is also true for 'experience': one cannot derive the idea of experience from that of action, whether it be referred to physical or to psychological events. Experiences concerning elementary particles show specific behaviors of physical energy that are attributed to certain beings, but in themselves these particles *are not* directly experienced. Maybe one could speak of the "Big Bang" and its consequences as a physical experience, so that scientific experiments would be minor imitations of it; but in such ways of thinking, the phrase 'physical experience' would be the transfer and extension of an anthropological behavior to the physical universe. I do not say that such a philosophy is unconceivable. Its marked anthropomorphism would require serious justifications; and the physical world would no longer be what it is supposed to be today—a set of objects in causal interaction.

Inversely, to establish an analogy between experience and construction and to see in the human mind a power of conceptual organization does not prove that the idea of experience comes from that of mental construction. For example, when Lakatos writes, "Mathematics, this product of human activity, 'alienates itself' from the human activity which has been producing it. It becomes a living, growing organism that acquires a certain autonomy from the activity which has produced it,"[24] his vision of mathematics as construction produced by human activity calls for the help of a genetic vision, which means that he postulates an analogy between human and biological activities. That is acceptable insofar as Man is seen as part of Nature; but that analogical assimilation between construction and organization is attached to the undefined concept of activity. To say that experience is a specific product of human activity is to satisfy ourselves with a vague semantic correspondence. In order to change an activity into an experience, something more is used; but what? Nobody says what it is. I can follow Peirce and state that any human action is experience. Then I suppose that you and I understand what we mean by experience that is more than simple physical or human action. Again, what is it?

I shall not take the example of scientific experimentation because I would be unable to conceive a scientific activity that is not an experiment or part of one. Let us consider simple cases with the understanding that our conclusion will have to be tested on scientific experimentations. Furthermore, I decide that the words 'experience' and 'experiment' will be used with no specific differentiation, as we have discarded the concept of "passive experience." Let us imagine that I decide to go to the local shopping center to buy food. It is a standard human action. It deals with an immediate future; it obeys a specific final system (the maintenance of my health by bodily nourishment); it implies instrumentation (I can walk, I can use my car, I can call a taxi, etc.). Then, if I add, "today I should experiment the new grocery store I heard about," my projected action takes on a new meaning or, more exactly, a new meaning is added to the basic one. It shows that I can treat an action as an experience, and in my mind the difference is clear. Now, let us imagine that, at the beginning of a class, I say to my students: "This course will be an experiment in post-structural analysis." By this I imply that my teaching, whatever it may be, will have an experimental character for me and my students. It will be intellectual training, and I cannot guarantee the results, my success as well as the consequences on my students' minds. I mean also that I am trying to escape the usual routine of literary teaching. In this second example, there is no dissociation between action and experience. My pedagogical activity is understood by itself as experience; but this time, I insist on the experimental character of a certain kind of intellectual experience. Thus, my question, "What is new in this instance?" echoes the question of the first example, "What is new this time about going to the store?"

It is not a change of routine, because I could change my habits without considering it an experiment, although the sense of novelty seems to be a precondition for initiating an experience in my daily life as well as in my intellectual meditations; but it is not the novelty of an act. A new course is not necessarily a new experiment in teaching. When I say, "It will be an experiment," I add a new dimension to my daily or professional actions in the sense that I isolate an act in the series of my deeds; it gets a special value independently of the usual values governing my actions. It means that at the same time I wish to evaluate an act in a certain case and actually to compare it with my preceding ones in order to make a decision concerning their own efficiency. In other words, this special act I call 'experience' is considered as a possible and future model, except if I judge to the contrary and return to my routine. Even in this conclusion, at least for a moment, my action was tested in view of a new shaping of my future. Then, to make an experience is to *remodel* the forms of my life in any situation and in such a way that I will be able to evaluate the new form under consideration. This last condition is important and should be emphasized. The development of an action does not become experience by itself and solely by my decision. It is slightly or deeply modified in regard to the consciousness of modeling. For instance, I will "test" the quality of the food, prices, facilities offered in buying and paying, its location, and reach a list of pros and cons on which to build up my future decisions and actions. In the same manner, the testing of a special course will develop itself with parallel controls, a similar ending and a reshaping of my professional activity. I cannot say that at any rate courses should be evaluated by instructors or students or that, if I am a good shopper, I should test any of my errands. It means that experiencing can become an intimate part of acting, although it does not mean that acting is inevitably experiencing.

Now we can turn to scientific experiences in all their forms and degrees. Contrary to a tradition nourished by two centuries of empiricism, induction is not the basic form of scientific thought. Not that such a way of reasoning is not used. Far from it, but it belongs to the universal decision of experiencing, especially to statistical experiencing when it is needed. Otherwise, as the most recent philosophies of science have correctly shown in reversing the empiricist trend, true scientific process is not the right to generalize and to propose inductive laws but the modeling of physical reality (I speak here as a realist scientist) thanks to those more and more powerful models called laboratory measuring instruments. For instance, new particles in atomic physics are similar to declarations of birth done by the experimenter after specific results of experience. The naming, in its baptismal act, is a conclusion of a physical modeling and an element within a model. Peirce was right in underlining the fact that scientific processes are not to be confused with any kind of human action: they are, he says, human action par excellence and distinct from any other form. Unfortunately his meditation stopped there. He did not explore the semantic relation between experience and model. Maybe was he too anxious to transform the realist belief into philosophical dogma!

Have we made some progress in our endeavor to confront the ideas of function and experience? First, there is no experiencing, that is, modeling-of-reality (the dashes are put to eliminate the implications of the realist postulate) without the awareness of a *correspondence* between two or more elements and without a *rule* making the experience possible. I must go further than that statement, because, contrary to what has been said since Locke and up until the myth of sensory data was destroyed, an experience is not the description of an association of endured and passive images. It is the shaping of the unknown or the less known into a model in such a way that, within it, elements play the respective roles of images and preimages. The most abstract scheme $y = f(x)$, is thus the model for less abstract models. The discrete parts $(x, y, \ldots)$, called elements of a set $A$, receive a shaping by the universal rule of correspondence, so that one element is subordinated to the other and in that way, is called image of the other. 'Image' has not the usual and concrete sense of reflection and representation of an object, but the sense of 'corresponding to' and, more precisely, of *being put into correspondence by a rule* that governs the most abstract model I can conceive, that is, the modeling of the most universal relation between the two phrases 'set of elements' and 'elements of set.'

The two consciousnesses of experience and function are thus quasi identical. To decide to do an experiment is to test a function in given circumstances, be it shopping, teaching, or studying atomic energy. *An experience is reality immediately understood as a function, as an operational model.* There is no other possible model than a function, a being-as-function and also a function-as-being. Then we understand the full significance of that first definition proposed in a textbook of mathematical analysis. Defining the word 'function' after implying the intuitive meaning of 'set' and 'element,' that is, accepting the mathematical symbols $A$, $x$ and $x \varepsilon A$, is doing more than naming and describing it. It is *making of a word a possible experience,* the point of departure of series of experiences and a rule of existence by which the object 'function' is identical to its operational power. In that perspective, mathematics is nothing less nor more than the *universal experience of language* by itself reducing its referent to a set of elements. Maybe the reason for the extension of mathematics to any domain of existence lies here, as well as the reason why scientific progress is duly assimilated to the mathematization of language. I did not need to lean on a realist or idealist philosophy of mathematics to explain its multiple applications from physics to all sorts of technologies; I only had to *expose* the quasi-identity of function and experience within language life and a minimal referential structure. Let us go a step further. If experience and function in their joint meaning cannot be derived from the concepts of Being, Mind, or Action, the only solution left would consist in understanding and living them as *fundamental concepts of language: before being applied to so-called independent referents, they express language in its living essence and its conditioning of reference.* One can speak of mathematical, physical, biological, sociological functions and experiences only because by itself language *is* experience-and-function, that is, manifests itself *as* experience and function. Thus, to speak of "linguistic experience" or "linguistic function" is pleonastic and only acceptable in an attempt to underline the universality of that kind of experience and function in opposition to the regionality of any other kind, even of the mathematical function that tends to serve as linguistic model for the other fields of knowledge and action.

Two last difficulties should be stated. First, is my writing really free from the belief in ontological referents? Even if we have substituted 'language' for 'being,' we continue to use the verb 'to be.' When I write "language is . . ." am I not implying the existence of an independent referent called "language" and thus positing that language is a being with specific qualities? If I succeeded in eliminating the psy-referent, do I reject the secret presence of the ontological referent, whatever it may be? Can I believe that 'is' is not ontologically loaded? There is one only answer: "is" would be a sort of linguistic appropriation, a linguistic experience-and-function. My statement concerning language has a reversible property: it should be read both ways: "language is experience-and-function" and "experience-and-function is language." 'Is' really means "equivalent to." It is not surprising that in the textbook of mathematical analysis I consulted earlier, the second definition, the one coming after that of function, is that of *equivalent relation,* introducing into mathematical language the reflective, symmetric, and transitive properties and thus specifying that 'is' designates a sort of relation: "If $R$ is a relation in $X$, we write $x \sim y$ provided $(x, y) \varepsilon R$ (where $\sim$ means 'related' and $\varepsilon$ 'belonging')." The mathematical application shows that 'is' is not a relation between a substance and its attributes or qualities. As I have stressed more than once, grammar is not parallel to logic, nor logic to ontology. This is the case in physics (at least in its modern achievements), and physicalism is no more than the trivial extension of physical application of language to any kind of application. Let us say again, that we are never forced to confuse the linguistic and the ontological powers of a proposition. When I *write,* "language is experience-and-function," I do not fall into a linguistic hypothetical substantialism. On the contrary, I issue for me and my reader a strong *warning: think language and function within themselves and with no other help.*

Then comes the second difficulty. *Writing,* as I did, "language is experience-and-function" is itself language and in this case language on language. Thus, my own writing is experience-and-function, referring to a linguistic experience-and-function. Here we come across the problem of the "speech act" within the perspective of language-experience. The statement "language is experience-and-function," like many others, comes as a conclusion or a relay among a painstaking effort in writing—a part in an experience of writing. It is obvious that writing the above sentence does not imply first thinking something true and writing about it later. Directly and truthfully I write such a statement because it follows analyses on the word 'function' and more generally is part of a patient endeavor to "uncap" linguistic implications. Indeed, it can happen that writing follows a certain experience and registers on paper results of experience done by specific instruments although, even in these cases, writing is always an indissociable part of the experimental language of—let us say—an astronomer or a chemist. Can we imagine a telescope without its preliminary description? The case of the philosopher is slightly different: philosophy is *actual and immediate experience in writing*. As such, it is constantly threatened by the confusion of experience and habits, innovation and repetition, integration and looseness. There are different levels of linguistic experience, and many adjectives qualify them: superficial or deep, light or serious, well articulated or dispersed, coherent or incoherent, and so on. The typed or printed form of a writing is just the final phase of many tries, hesitations, corrections, even when a written dialogue plays at being a former oral event. Furthermore, a writer is always secretly and at times desperately conscious of the contingency of his writings. What he writes could have been something else, other words, other turns of phrase. It is why a philosopher often feels that he is experimenting on himself in unpredictable and contingent manners.

Coming back to the writing of the sentence, "Language is experience-and-function," I know that it occurs at the end of this meditation, but that it is more than a summing up. It is part of my writing modified by it, and it has to be repeated just to obtain a better consolidation of the new universe it belongs to—a universe where the word 'reference' learns to live without its usual crutches. I know also that it has to be experienced in its consequences. It invites a reorganization of the relation between the main concepts language invents to experiment on itself. It suggests a new critical *exposition* of the most important implications that make up linguistic life in its enormous complexity.

# MEDITATION FIVE

## *Existing as Reference*

What does it mean to experience language at any moment of my life and any level of its actions, but without the philosophical support of the realist postulate, or R-postulate, the psy-referent, and the F-function? Let me repeat it doggedly: I believe no more in the existence of referents waiting for my search of their significations; I do not refer those semantic endeavors to an I responsible for them; I do not claim that my linguistic commitments are parts of myself as acting being; I just know that I am language aware of itself and experiencing itself. If I find out no justifications for independent referents, I still feel reference as a fundamental need, but a need that is more or less satisfied, more or less fit to establish and control a world of referents. I know also that what centuries of idealist philosophies have called "consciousness" is not a psychological reality but a universal and intimate aspect of my referential life, which develops itself as *explicitation of the implicit:* to refer is to explicit something implied, so that the relation of implication is the universal law of my references and the source for any other relation, especially the causal and final relations. Thus to apprehend reference in itself is to become aware of my personal life as explicitating the implied under the species of the sign and to give to that expression a certain existential and intellectual quality, a value. This is why to refer is always at the same time to evaluate oneself and the world, *to be critical.*

My working program goes beyond my own capacities. A new referential fever is possessing me. I have already put on my agenda the rewriting of the relation of reference with perception and memory. However, before undertaking this Herculean cleaning, and just to give myself, and eventually my reader, a little more confidence, for a while I plan to meditate on the double experience of referential explicitation and critic.

### *Explicitating the Implicit*

At the end of the first meditation, I discovered philosophical meditation as "exposition of implications," as "empirical awareness of what I presuppose each time I raise a problem, choose a method, or offer a solution." At the end of a slow process, which "exposed" what I believed to be the basic implications of theories of language in modern thought, I come to understand that the "problem of language" should become a simultaneous meditation of, on, and by three words: *experience, function, reference.* I am also realizing that *the linguistic process is nothing more than the process of implicitation-explicitation:* there is no living language without an attempt to elaborate implicitations into explicitations; and there is no explicitation without a rich, almost inexhaustible domain of implied thoughts, thoughts that are not enunciated, but support the enunciation to be. Is it not revealing that Plato and many other philosophers after him identified thought and reminiscence, and that modern logicians have stated that any proposition is related to the infinite propositions comprehending the "universe of discourse?"

There is also a subtle relation between the adjective 'implicit' and the verb 'to imply' or its substantive form 'implicitation': paradoxically 'to imply' designates the presence of something implicit, but at the same time, it recognizes it, it explicits it. This is why there is no language and thus, no reference, without the awareness of implicit thinking and also a complex system of implicit marking, surrounding languages of Being, Mind, and Action. When modern logicians introduced implicitation as part of the basic operations of their calculus (for instance, B. Russell positing the distinction of *material* and *formal implications*), they formalized a great number of expressions of our common languages, such as "if you say that . . . you suppose that . . . , you mean that . . . , you hint, you suggest, you leave unsaid, you insinuate, you concede, you presuppose, you assume, you presume." The algorithm '$a \rightarrow b$' simultaneously concerns beings such as classes, relations, propositions. It is also read as "meaning *a,* I imply *b*" or "I refer to *b*." That is language, its original and permanent expression, in its power of explicitation.

The passage from implicit to explicit or, better said, the *explicitation of the implicit,* has a modal quality: it is felt, asserted, as necessary or possible. Scientific theories or philosophical meditations tend to show how a contingent implication is actually necessary, by means of logical, mathematical, or experimental proofs. In an ideal limit, knowledge, fully achieved, would be the total exposition of linguistic implications: an ideal impossible to reach although from generation to generation philosophers make generous attempts at it—Leibniz and Hegel having offered to the Western world the most fantastic organizations of the implicit for modern languages, ending in the apotheosis of the principle of Preestablished Harmony or the Concept totalizator, as triumphs of the Implicit-Explicited!

Obviously the two ideas of function and implicitation are closely connected. Together they help to refer to Being and Action. The functional correspondence between *x* and *y*, or the idea of relation in its universality, are themselves "implying" that they cannot be put into languages without the awareness of a linguistic passage from the implicit to the explicit: "*a*" implies "*b*" leads to "*a* is a function of *b*." In a similar fashion, concepts of faculty, power, virtuality have lived and developed within that passage that makes of the "consciousness of something" the awareness of an explicitation inviting the search for an actual implicitation. We can maybe risk saying that many of the theoretical difficulties encountered by Western philosophies since Plato and Aristotle come from the fact that the language of the Implicit-Explicit was commonly interpreted in terms of ontological and pragmatic languages or with the theory of reminiscence omnipresent in our epistemologies.

Following the preceding trend of our meditation, and with no pretense to a hasty explanation, I shall be conscious of the 'implicit-explicit' as the fundamental linguistic experience: *to expose is to organize a world where the two universal modes of existence are the implicit and the explicit; to be language is to experience oneself as an alternation of expression and silence, that is, of explicitation and implicitation,* which is why we very often feel that *we are more and/or less than we are saying and writing; our temporal life between past and future presupposes the deepest rhythm of making beings and things implicit and explicit. To use a well-referred to expression of Western metaphysics, the rhythm of the explicit and the implicit is governed by the hidden and unmasked God of reference.*

Before making a pause may I make one last effort of concentration and repetition in order to emphasize the main changes I am trying to introduce in *my personal awareness of language.* I hope that those changes will modify the common way of referring to our linguistic behaviors and will help especially to *expose* the implicitations lying behind our daily experience of speaking and writing. Such exposures should finally contribute to uncap and counteract the transparency effect by which languages expect to trick themselves, and to lose themselves in the oral and written projections of their referents:

—*Philosophy is meditation on language by way of language.* Any attempt to go beyond that linguistic reversion belongs to science, to universal or regional ontologies. The traditional search for philosophical systematization—absolute or partial gatherings of languages into systems—results from a permanent contamination of meditation and science. From Descartes on, modern thought has put itself into the contradictory situation of making of science the only acceptable knowledge, yet requiring a philosopher to *say* it! Not pretending to be a scientist of the prime or the last order, I assert that to meditate is to feel the presence of language in its own rising and life. Consequently, meditation refuses to categorize itself under any other word. It establishes itself at the center of everything. To take a well-known distinction, meditation is neither constative nor performing. It is—pardon me this easy pun—medi(t)ating.

—Insofar as linguistics is the science of language, it requires a belief in *linguistic determinism* and in the existence of *laws* governing the production of languages. Nonetheless, such a belief should not be assimilated with physical determinism, at least as it is understood today. Indeed, any language obeys constants, repetitions, rules of transformation; but there is no absolute linguistic necessity. One can speak of a *contingent determinism*. Any language could have been different from what it is, not by virtue of statistical determinism but because it is its own invention and as such, unforeseeable. For instance, the French language, as it developped from its origins, was unpredictable for the same reason as Racine or Stendhal's writings were unconceivable before their occurrences.

—The most widespread concept of "natural languages," used without malice, almost inadvertantly, should be banished. It is purely trivial to imply that language is part of human nature or of nature in general (for example, in a semiotic perspective). It only gives a superficial solution to a crucial problem. To favor Naturalism—a convenient and comfortable shelter for philosophers—is to entertain a banal theoretical illusion.

—*The naturalistic illusion* often involves the alibi of the linguistic *brain model*, but it draws from it no positive information except for a very vague promise that one day a neuropsychologist theory of language will be achieved. Indeed, it does not say how, in that distant future, cerebral energy will be understood in its diverse localizations and functions. It is a convenient and safe decision that unfortunately leads nowhere. There is only one sensible solution for someone who thinks that neurophysiology is the exclusive region where one should discuss language in valuable terms: to study neurophysiology and to denounce as unacceptable any other attempt at explaining language. Even with such a drastic reduction, the ultimate question of the relation of the brain's organization and language would not be solved. Between the two following propositions, "brain is the cause of language" and "language is the cause of brain," is there a choice? Neurophysiology by itself is unable to justify its "natural" option in favor of a cerebral causal power that is supposed to produce languages.

—The classical philosophical theories called *Realism, Idealism, Spiritualism,* and *Pragmatism* are not only beyond any kind of verification and demonstration but *they are unable to take into account the actual existence of language.* The belief in a Being other than language, in a Mind source of language, in the universality of what I proposed calling F-function, is an endeavor to explain language with something that is not language. It leaves us standing before two mysteries: *"how can language speak about something that is not language?"* and *"how can something that is not language be at the origin of language?"* These philosophical difficulties cannot allow us to forget the omnipresence in our languages—be they common, scientific, literary, or philosophical—of three linguistic systems that invade the most elaborate and the most simple of our linguistic behaviors—the language of Being (the R-postulate), the language of Mind (the psy-referent), and the language of Action (the F-function). Once we are rid of the philosophical generalizations that orchestrate them, we, new ploughmen of language, should till their grounds.

At this moment in my writing, my meditation should be able to take on a positive turn. It is no longer necessary to continue to pronounce caveats and to denounce arbitrary philosophical postulations. Uncapping efforts should have produced some effects on our linguistic habits and our general attitude toward language. At least, in a very subjective way, I feel that my intimacy with language is changed. I have acquired a new consciousness of language without the dubious support of the psy-referent. I should be ready for the next step: to live and to write about linguistic power within the confrontation of reference, perception, and imagination.

One last scruple and reticence after so many pages devoted to word cleaning and housekeeping: To invite guests does not usually mean inviting them to share in the keeping of your house! All these pages fighting alleged errors, do they not express a very naive intellectual arrogance? Should my direct apprehension of language really begin now? Surely, nothing can stop my eventual readers from bypassing those preliminaries. I can give one only excuse (if it is one) for the slowness of my critical process: as a retarded philosopher, I know how long it took me to arrive at this moment of linguistic awareness and philosophical independence. I have also progressively realized that one of Descartes pieces of advice in the *Discourse on Method* was of vital importance: *Do not be rash!* In the present rush and cult for speed, even in intellectual research, such advice should be received as a daily practice of the interior life and the true tension of meditation. The duty of nonprecipitation applies to the critical effort to slow down the impulse to believe; it is also an endless culture of patience and of humour in its will to be candid. One will never know if one has been patient enough, if the wait for word organization has been long enough. Maybe tomorrow it would have been better. On the other hand, Pascal tells us that you cannot postpone the time of commitment, that you can die tonight! Do you expect to keep God waiting for your decision? Decision about what? I do not doubt that language exists at this very moment I am writing that it exists. I put a distance within my language, making it an exercise of suspension, between absence and presence; but I can no longer stay in this neutral limbo, because language is my life, more than instrument for life, life itself as it is experienced. I do not have to decide if God, the world, the human mind exist: *the problem of their existence as independent referent is illusory*. We know it now. I know also that I cannot live without language, which is then my only reality and measure of reality, my only food, giving to any other referent its universal existential condition. All my decisions should imply this question: *How can I live the existence of God, of the world, of myself as mind through the life of language in myself, with myself, and outside myself?* Such is the problem of reference, emerging now, liberated from its practical and theoretical implications. Linguists have been obsessed by the "meaning of meaning" and yet have not succeeded in freeing themselves from all sorts of philosophical implications. Being conscious of that state of affairs, am I able to meditate on the *reference to reference* as the permanent tension of my present intellectual life? Such is my decision, and my wager: I decide not to believe in God or in the universe, not even in myself, but to believe that *reference is my existence, my existence is reference; all conditions abolished, my past and present writing is my only reference.*

## *Reference as Existing and Evaluating Energy*

After those cautious, slow, and painful movements of writing within language, after becoming more and more aware that any effort to jump out of the linguistic universe is vain and only means a twisting of language on itself, in this new state of negations, restraints and constraints, which hopes to be a true radicalization of the millenary skeptical revolts, in a domain of pure existence through writing, which gives rise to a strange crepuscular light where meanings are not well separated one from the other, I perceive a few ideas flickering, and among them, a sort of existential assurance: *to exist is to refer to.* Reference *is the* way of being as well as being *is the* way of reference. I am forced to play with that fundamental reversing, but never forgetting that if 'being' is the universal and unique referent, it is because it is required by reference. In simple phrasing, 'referent' implies reference as its basic existence, but reference does not exist because referents are waiting for it, if not within any reference life. Godot has no transcendent existence but in Beckett's writings.

In the same manner language does not instigate domains of meanings expecting their indexation by referents. On the contrary, language is the dynamics of reference elaborating specific meanings. Frege had an inspired presentiment of that primordial fact; and one day I will have to reconsider in detail his famous essays. In the meanwhile I must remain attached to my first act of positive faith: *I write, therefore I refer to,* which, to discard the fallacy of a deductive process, should be written: *"Writing, I refer to."*

This new reading of the Cartesian *Cogito* entails the rejection of the belief in a thinking substance, be it spiritual or material. What I have called a psy-referent is but a contingent consequence of the human referential life. Writing calls for a *I* writing, not the opposite. It is not enough to say with Merleau-Ponty that 'I' belongs to the "adventures of dialectics." Merleau-Ponty remained idealist in spite of himself. It must be said that the 'I' is part of the vicissitudes of referential research. Becoming an 'I' is a specific way of referring to, that is of existing. Emile Benveniste was right in positing the subjective anchorage of language, but it seems that he did not realize that subjectivity was required by language itself, not by a preexisting mind.

Indeed these flickers of understanding need much more meditative exploration. I will have to rewrite and to recondition my usual and philosophical languages. I can already anticipate the new interrogations to which I will have to redirect my critical reflection. Actually these new problems concern old problems that I should reinstate along my new intellectual obligation, that is basically, to refuse to think with the help of postulates traditionally accepted by philosophers and scientists. From now on, it is clear that the classical problems of *perception, memory, judgment* call for a radical reformulation. Since my only experience is reference, what does it mean to write, "I see a tree in my garden"? What does it mean to write, "I remember seeing a tree in my garden"? What does it mean to write, "I certify that there is (was) a tree in my garden"? To put it briefly, the functions of perception, memory, and judgment must be rewritten in terms of reference, as aspects of human referential life.

That situation will be the same for a new understanding of literary and artistic life as well as for the consciousness of my present writing. The title given to my first meditations *The Imagination of Reference* requires a clarification. Many a reader have likely guessed why I chose such a cover for those meditations, and why I decided to postpone temporarily the critical examination of the word 'imagination.' Indeed that word is supposed to act as a preliminary warning, a sort of flashing red light at the entrance of my philosophical road. To declare from the beginning that reference belongs to the universe of the Imaginary is prohibiting any attempt to rely on the R-postulate. Surely it is also assuming the risk of reducing language life to an indefinite game of artificial combinations. I am ready to accept that risk, if, at least for a moment, the presence of the word 'imagination' neutralizes the effects of the realist assurance. Furthermore, reaching the end of these first meditations, I should take care not to fall into the snare of the psy-referent, that is, to fall back into the belief in the existence of a universal psychological power called 'imagination.' For me, in my present state of mind, 'imagination' and 'imaginary' depend on the life and labor of reference. One day I will have to understand how the human referential life feels the need for basic psychological oppositions such as imagination/perception, imagination/memory, imagination/reality, and so on in order to understand also why in the wake of the seventeenth-century suspicion toward imagination, the following centuries made of it the fundamental source of human creativity. In the meanwhile, 'imagination' will have helped me to apprehend 'reference' in its full autonomy and power within the universe of my writing.

The word 'power' just came in a very simple manner with the spontaneous movement of my writing. It implies that my referential life is governed by a sort of linguistic energy. Not that I go back surreptitiously to a shameful physicalism transferred to language itself! On the contrary, physical energy, as written by atomic physics, could be considered as deriving from linguistic energy; but for the moment let us not get involved in that paradoxical semantic game! Being liberated from my cultural postulations, I feel language as a power of reference that has its degrees of expression, its more or less powerful existential moments. Our referential life is made of long periods of routine responses with low significance, separated by sudden suspenses of intense moments when reference reaches its peak for right or wrong reasons. These moments of reference in their becoming are as varied as human experience can be: avowal of love, statement under oath, poetic explosion, intellectual insights, exceptional instants in reading and writing, and so on. Needless to say, between alterations of routine and intensity there are indefinite degrees of referential existence; for example, the understanding of a physical law by a trained physicist or by a secondary-school student, the contemplation of a work of art by an artist (Picasso looking at El Greco) and by an art lover. When with a savage humour Albert Camus writes, "Quinze mille francs par mois, la vie d'atelier et Tristan n'a plus rien à dire à Yseult." [Fifteen thousand francs monthly, workshop life, and Tristan does not have anything more to say to Yseult anymore], he expresses the tragedy of love in our industrial societies in terms of referential discourse, the failure of language creativity, and its inevitable erosion.

Evoking that complex domain of interrelations between the individual and collective selves and their languages, am I sending back the theory of reference to psycho-linguistics, thus surreptitiously restoring the psy-referent? On the contrary, I suggest that psycho-linguistics should be entirely revised and newly founded along the present conclusions on the unicity and universality of reference as linguistic energy in its extreme variations and indefinite degrees. The basic problem is not, as in current psycho-linguistics, "how does mind react to language?" but "how does language make a human being exist as mind?" My readers may remember that in the first meditation I recommend that the study of language should never remain at the level of routine usage but should always stay aware of language at its most innovative moments. That advice remains even more imperative at the end of my critical endeavor of linguistic and conceptual mine sweeping after we have become conscious of language as referential power with variable intensities, unpredictable qualities, artistic creativity or inertia, as style of being oneself and the other in a unique experience by which metaphysical reflection is meditative writing.

## *For a New Kind of Critical Thinking: Reference Criticism*

At last I have become aware of my personal life as a referential life with its ups and downs, its joys and pains, its exhilarations and dull moments, its feelings of presence and absence, its fullness and emptiness, its instants of cheerfulness and of dejection, its search for communion and its estrangements. I could rewrite Amiel's or Maine de Biran's *Journals* in that perspective and as tragic stories of reference. May I remember one day of my referential life: waking up: the interior monolog goes out of its dreaming periods; I reassume myself and my usual world of references as if I were preparing and encouraging my body to start a new day of presence to my self-and-the-World (in the first pages of *Swan's Way* (*Du Côté de chez Swann*) Proust gave the most powerful expression of that daily reaffirmation of references in human life); washing, dressing, breakfast: little by little I feel stronger, more committed; I feel reinstated, ready to project my stream of language into actions, ready to ascertain new references; sitting at my desk, looking at yesterday's writings, correcting them, improving their referential quality, beginning new pages; what I call absentmindedly the exterior world tends to fade out; I try to take possession of what I call ideas through the writing of words; the intensity of my concentration may vary, but with continuous heed I am looking for a text that expresses with more or less success a continuous state of reference; I feel more real than ever, although at times I go over periods of doubt and irresolution: maybe my writing is displaying a world of illusory references; then I call for rules and criteria that should help me to give to my references a sort of confirmation before affronting the others' confirmations or disapprovals. That kind of remembrance of past references could go on indefinitely.

The preceding paragraph *refers to* the beginning of a day for a man—myself—who finds the solution to his referential life through philosophical writing. Indeed there are thousands of other ways of looking for reference and of fulfilling oneself in human life, although all of them are aspects of language. It is not proper to discuss now their respective importance, if there is any! Societies are made of artificial hierarchies in reference. Finally it always comes back to myself, to my own feeling of existing-and-understanding, of *referring to as existence ascertaining or doubting its value*. I can specify the value of my reference, and say that my language is true, or expressive, or bringing moral exhortations, or even revealing. However, behind those particular qualifications, there is a general quality common to the values recognized by Western philosophies, the value of reference, or in less ambiguous phrasing, *reference as value experience*. In Kantian terms one could say that the three *Critiques,* to which one should add *Religion within the limits of Reason,* should be integrated into and founded on a unique and universal *Critique of Reference*.

Maybe the present philosophical confusion of the Western mind can be explained by such a state of affairs—philosophies no more able to say what

Truth, Good, Beauty, the Sacred, mean, assimilating one to the other, feeling that, beyond their specific values, they should call for a universal value that makes possible and sustains their attempts to build up languages of Truth, of Beauty, of Good, of Revelation. Aware of such a situation one could also understand our present epistemological and axiological perplexities in front of the relations between science and art, theory and practice, explanation and interpretation. Furthermore, all along our century there has been a recurrent cultural lamentation concerning the so-called crisis of the Humanities becoming unable to know what they are and what their purposes in the education of modern societies can be. More and more frequently educators of all ranges deplore the nihilistic turn taken by criticism (mainly by art and literary criticism) with its invitation to textual deconstruction, even destruction; these good souls often advocate a return to the defense of traditional moral values to give back to languages and social behaviors following them the stability that modern societies have lost. I sympathize with these generous intents, but I am afraid that they do not reach the core of our cultural crisis. What is called deconstructionism in its diverse garbs has had and certainly continues to have its raison d'être. Modern tongues have become aware of the manipulating and mystifying powers of contemporary ways of speaking and writing, thus of the obligation to expose false principles, ambiguous values, devious reasonings, treacherous mythologies. In my own judgment, and in spite of deconstructionism's present weaknesses, that sort of criticism is sustained by a legitimate and still valid intent. However, because of poor and inefficient techniques, it has mishandled the Nietzschean call for "transvaluation" in our modernity; it has not understood that above all the problem of value is the problem of value reference, that is, of language's referential energy.

This is why I believe that deconstructionism cannot be hastily replaced by one does not know what moral or ideological correctness, or by dictatorial codes based upon limited referents such as race, class, myth, gender, and so on. The present meditation leads us toward the instauration of a *reference criticism,* which will not claim to absorb literature and the arts into a final domain of critical comprehension, but which will attempt to evaluate, that is, to make us conscious of, the referential energy concentrated into any sort of texts and works of art. At the end of the twentieth century critical problems are no more "is there or not a moral message?" or "how have rhetoric codes been used in a correct or delusive manner?", or "how has a particular language been distorted?," or "how can psychoanalysis or Marxism intervene to explain the pros and cons of human praxis?," to mention only the main questions through which current criticism pretends to cover and evaluate the field of human creativity. The critical problem to face should be absorbed into a unique scrutiny: *what are the referential energy accumulated into language and the power of its effects when they are felt by hearers or readers*? It is clear that, when a language is well specified, that universal critical question is itself limited to the codes of that language: this is true for any sort of scientific and artificial language; but for any other language the reference question remains, primordial and preliminary. It is felt and expressed as soon as someone reacts to a given message in its fullness, and not only as a simple information.

New developments in literary and art criticism in our century have prepared the way for what I just proposed to call *reference criticism:* emphasis put on the text itself and its effects, not on its surroundings; search for its internal structure and sense of its unavoidable ambiguities; rejection of a simple relation of causality between author and work; and finally, with the denunciation of a rhetorical logocentrism, the awareness of all sorts of referential falsifications due to cultural and political accommodations. However, deconstructionism has failed in its great enterprise of linguistic purification and rectification. It has been accused of cutting down the tree of language on which it is perched. The main reason behind this disturbing cultural mess lies in a simple fact: all those critical questionings remain attached to the three postulates I tried to uncap and neutralize. The deconstructionist mistake does not lie in the outrageous belief in the unique reality of textism, as John Searle said about Jacques Derrida, but in the affirmation that reference presupposes a previous referent and that the fundamental function of language resides in the constitution of a well wrought universe of significations. The present call for ideological and ethical correctness is more dangerous than the evil it hopes to eliminate.

For any text or work of art reference criticism will try to expose its referential power, which will be felt as soon as it is perceived by the author or the recipient. It helps to solve the endemic problems that have overburdened criticism for centuries—the dualities of form and content, of philosophy and rhetoric—because the experience of reference is at the same time search for existence and understanding through and by language. For example, when Albert Camus wrote *L'Etranger,* he did not simply hope to add a new character to the collection of those who appear in Western contemporary novels: such a wish would be of secondary importance! Only in an indirect manner does he delivers to his potential readers a moral message concerning the death penalty in France and the biased attitudes of

French judges. He does not insist on the brilliance of his new narrative techniques. Indeed all these intents are present, but they are implied in a deeper exigency that directly concerns himself writing along the three rhetorical possibilities of novel, theater, and essay. Doing so he gave to the French language, in its literary capacity, new referential powers that will reverberate among his numerous readers. Important critics have brilliantly analyzed his grammar, his style, his art of thematic development, not realizing that they were exposing Camus's varied techniques for introducing referential possibilities that Meursault, as imaginary referent, incarnates. *L'Etranger* offers thus more than a new psychology of characters. It is a deep revolution in the way language is able to give existence to individuals; it is also a new type of reference between people. Many critics saw in Meursault the portrait of the anonymous creature, a pitiful product of our modern societies. For want of understanding Camus's discovery of a revolutionary referential language, many critics went wrong. Meursault, and some of his successors like Beckett's Molloy, Malone, even Worm, are not sad derelicts, precursors of the homeless people, or the ferocious and lucid caricatures of our own images and behaviors. They are true innovators who initiate the references they "deserve." When Camus said that Meursault was "the Christ we deserve," he had a presentiment of reference criticism. His hero rediscovered for our era the revolutionary language of the Gospel.

For a second test, let us read two fragments of René Char's poetry. Char is the true descendant of Baudelaire, who, as we saw, intensively explored the poetic effects of the psy-referent within the lexical triplet "interior-invisible-reflective"; but the author of *Fureur et mystère* belongs to a period that began to restore language to its direct referential powers and to understand that the Verb is not instrument of thought but revelation at any level of the human individual and collective existence:

> La poésie est à la fois parole et provocation silencieuse, désespérée de notre être—exigeant pour la venue d'une réalité qui sera sans concurrence.
>
> [Poetry is at the same time voice and silent provocation, despairing of our being—demanding the coming of a reality that will be without competition.] (*La Parole et l'archipel*)[1]

> Nos paroles sont lentes à nous parvenir, comme si elles contenaient, séparées, une sève suffisante pour rester close tout un hiver; ou mieux, comme si, à chaque extrémité de la silencieuse distance, se mettant en joue,

il leur était interdit de s'élancer et de se joindre. Notre voix court de l'un à l'autre; mais chaque avenue, chaque treille, chaque fourré, la tire à lui, la retient, l'interroge. Tout est prétexte à la ralentir.

[Our words are slow to reach us, as if separated, they hold in enough sap to stay sealed one winter long; or better, as if at each end of the silent distance, taking aim at themselves, they were prohibited to soar up and to join. Our voice runs from one to the other; but each avenue, each vine-trellis, each thicket draws it, detains it, questions it. Everything is pretext to slow it.] (*La Parole et l'archipel*)[2]

In these two texts, 'poetry' writes and tells us what poetry is, that is, 'poetry.' The poem institutes and constitutes poetry through itself (auto-referentiality, as it has been said). Actually any saying—and all the more so any writing—refers to itself and to oneself, double and fundamental experience of the same and the other, as philosophers and poets have known and written for two millenaries. Char's first text tells the poet anxious to convert his or her existence into the subsistence and power of certain words to which from now on his or her existence will refer. The verb 'être', ('to be') seems to give the sentence the aspect of a functional definition. However, if the reader makes of his or her reading an identification of his or her life to the text read, he or she will understand that the F-function of language is overcome: by *'est'* ('is'), Char designates a 'being language' in specific conditions. The poet is not an I-substance but an I-demanding and anguished by his own demand. What demand? The "coming of reality." Clearly the R-postulate is put aside: 'reality' intervenes as something that arrives, introduced by the poetic reference; it is the basic referent required by poetry, never the support of poetry. This sort of "good news" implies the great surrealist dream: reality is a moment and place of communion realized by poetic writing or reading. The universal opposites that dominate languages will be subdued by the poet, or more exactly, by the actual sentence putting reference into being. Briefly Char's apparent definition of poetry is a declaration of poetic reference where and when words and silences combine to become existence reconciled. Char, in a simple and unique movement of his writing exposes what I have painfully mastered—the life of language within language liberated from its current servitudes, from what I have called the R-postulate, the psy-referent, and the F-function.

The second text has the apparent aspect of a description, as if it were referring to a pre-existing state of poetic existence, implying thus the belief in a psy-referent. Actually it is not the case. The poet is living his own experience in writing poetry. Let us not be mystified! He does not intend to write the objective account of a psychological adventure. Language becomes conscious of itself as a slowing down process. Surrealist poets had already warned the users of poetic roads: "*Ralentir, Travaux!*" [Slow down, People at work]. One may remember the Cartesian warning against precipitation, but with a difference: Descartes recommended a permanent fight against the common hurry of the human mind. On the other hand, Char dreams of a speed without limit by which poetry reaches its highest moments; but poetry cannot avoid the fact of language slowing down. Language is itself a linguistic sap, concentrating, sleeping during the winters of referential life and breaking the stream of writing. The sap is referential power going into words and emprisoned by them so that the poet's voice "runs" from one to the other and finds all sorts of excuses to give to each selected word a special and unique existential power by which the poet allows himself to be elated.

More should be said about the tree-and-forest reference in a fully developed criticism. Let us only face a crucial problem: if, with a rare poetical instinct, Char avoids the trap of the psy-referent, is he not falling into the insidious trap of rhetoric beautification? Is he not speaking of poetry through a more or less traditional set of metaphors? Reference to sap and its circulation, to bushes, forests, and roads does not offer adequate comparisons, not even illuminating analogies. Char reverses the realist relation! He invites us to understand that the biological sap makes sense through the poetic reference of language in search for appropriate referents. Traditional rhetoric proposed concepts that obeyed Aristotelian realism. Surrealism restored poetry in its authentic quality. The relation between Char and Heidegger should not surprise the reader. The Heideggerian *Dasein* is near relative to Char's sap; but as we already noted, Heidegger did not succeed in disentangling his writing from the psy-referent. Char's writing does better and is one of the best examples for a life/writing that understands words as concentration of referential energy, and their dramatic assemblage as human existence at different levels of revelation.

After trying to show the new style of reference criticism, one may remember a piece of advice suggested at the beginning of the first meditation: to test language, do not imitate linguists with their artificial phrasings and sentences but look for languages where reference explodes in its novelty. I just referred to Camus and Char because, among a few others, they are great masters in reference: they contributed to the formation and learning of our referential lives, when those lives are not controlled by scientific or technological codes. One can also understand why in the second part of the twentieth century criticism has attempted to conquer all domains of language, as if creativity required to become aware of itself, and of reference, conscious of what it has been and continues to be for any tongue at any time of human prehistory and history. All over the world in our universities, the teaching of Humanities is deeply disturbed. Am I too arrogant in thinking that the Humanities are still too much embedded in old and modern philosophical frames that prevent them from reforming themselves and from finding the proper criticism that would give to the departments of languages and history their real unity and value? It is difficult to be rid of old habits and values which seem to help societies to pursue their jolting wanderings; but what is at stake is worth fighting for!

This is maybe my only excuse for such a lengthy and meandering piece of writing that has no beginning and no end—a piece of writing that should always be ready to start again the effort of uncapping the most powerful prejudices of our languages and to maintain our attention focused on a few vital caveats. This is not as easy to do as to build up perfect intellectual symmetries and provocative architectures; but after my loyal endeavors to test the new ideas on language and mind proposed by our century, I can but conclude that *reference criticism*[3] is the only way left open between the current deadlocks of discouraged and skeptical indifference, blinded and imperious dogmatisms, and pluralistic anarchy.

# *Notes*

## *Meditation One*

1. Maurice Merleau-Ponty, *Prose du monde,* p. 129.
2. Blaise Pascal, *Œuvres complètes,* fragment 683.
3. Stéphane Mallarmé, *Œuvres,* p. 418.
4. Mallarmé, *Œuvres,* p. 828.
5. André Martinet, *Eléments de linguistique générale,* p. 7.
6. George A. Miller. "Psychology and Communication" in *Communication, Language, and Meaning,* edited by G. A. Miller (New York: Basic Books, 1973), p. 3.
7. Ferdinand de Saussure, *Cours de linguistique générale,* p. 25.
8. Ibid., p. 25.
9. Ibid., pp. 267–68.
10. John Lyons, *Language and Linguistics,* p. 3.
11. Willard O. Quine, *Word and Object,* p. 3.
12. Mallarmé, *Œuvres,* p. 901.
13. André Meillet, *Introduction à l'étude comparée des langues indo-europeénnes,* p. 18.
14. Noam Chomsky, *Aspects of the Theory of Syntax,* pp. 2–3.
15. David Marr, *Vision,* p. 357.
16. Michel Bréal, *Essai de sémantique,* p. 7.
17. Ibid., p. 88.
18. Meillet, *Introduction à l'étude compareé,* p. 21 (italics mine).
19. *The Rig Veda,* p. 63.
20. Louis Renou, *Hymnes spéculatifs du Veda,* p. 71.
21. In Daniel C. Dennet's "Foreword" to Ruth Garrest Millikan's *Language, Thought and Other Biological Categories, New Foundations for Realism.*

## *Meditation Two*

1. John Searle, "On Deconstruction," *New York Review of Books,* October 27, 1983, pp. 874–79.
2. John Searle, *Intentionality: An Essay in the Philosophy of the Mind,* p. 158–59.
3. Hilary Putnam, *Reason, Truth and History,* p. 17.

4. Etienne Gilson, *Le Réalisme méthodique,* p. 88.

5. Martin Heidegger, *The Basic Problems of Phenomenology,* p. 214.

6. See Martin Heidegger, *Being and Time,* paragraph 18: "Involvement and Significance; the Worldhood of the World."

7. André Lalande, *Vocabulaire technique et critique de la philosophie,* 7th ed., "Realism."

8. Karl R. Popper and John C. Eccles, *The Self and Its Brain* (New York: Springer International, 1977), p. 9. Quoted in Ian Hacking, *Representing and Intervening,* pp. 145–46.

## *Meditation Three*

1. 1st edition, 1939; 5th edition, expanded, 1970.

2. "Bref l'idéalisme absolu nous apparaîtra comme la médiation intellectuelle par laquelle la philosophie peut entrer dans le spiritualisme" [In brief absolute idealism will appear to us as the intellectual mediation thanks to which philosophy is able to enter into spiritualism]. Ibid., p. 89.

3. Quoted in André Lalande, *Vocabulaire technique,* p. 440.

4. 1st edition, 1949.

5. See Hilary Putnam, *Mind, Language and Reality,* especially Chapters 20 and 21.

6. Nelson Goodman, *Of Mind and Other Matters,* Preface.

7. See Nelson Goodman, *Languages of Art: Approach to a Theory of Symbols,* p. 38.

8. Ibid., p. 264.

9. Ibid., p. 241.

10. Noam Chomsky, *Language and Mind,* pp. 1, 103.

11. Noam Chomsky, *Rules and Representations,* "Mind and Body," p. 9.

12. Georg Hegel, *Phenomenologie des Geistes,* p. 552: "Das Vollkommene Element, worin die Innerlichkeit eben so äusserlich als die Äusserlichkeit innerlich ist, ist wieder die Sprache."

13. Edited and translated by E. Hamfman and G. Vakar (New York: Wiley, 1962).

14. Samuel Beckett, *The Unnamable* (New York: Grove Press, 1958), p. 179. In French: "c'est peut-être un rêve . . . un silence de rêve, plein de murmures, je ne sais pas, ce sont des mots . . . c'est tout ce que je sais . . . ils m'ont peut-être déjà dit...dans le silence on ne sait pas. . . ." *L'Innommable* (Paris: Editions de Minuit, 1953), pp. 261–62.

15. *Henry James, The Art of the Novel* (New York: Scribner, 1934), pp. 31–32.

16. Stéphane Mallarmé, "Les Fenêtres," in *Œuvres Complétes,* p. 32.

17. Charles Baudelaire, "Bénédiction," in *Les Fleurs du mal,* (1st ed., 1857), p. 7.

18. Charles Baudelaire, "Les Fenêtres," in *Poèmes en Prose* (1st ed., 1862), p. 339.

19. "Le Miroir," in ibid., p. 344.

20. Ferdinand de Saussure, *Course in General Linguistics,* p. 16.

21. Samuel Beckett, *Compagnie,* pp. 87–88.

22. See Samuel Kripke, *Wittgenstein on Rules and Private Language.*

## *Meditation Four*

1. See "Act," in *Semantics of Natural Languages,* edited by Donald Davidson and Gilbert Hartman, p. 116.

2. André Martinet, *Eléments de linguistique générale,* p. 9.

3. Ibid., p. 12.

4. Michel Bréal, *Essai de sémantique,* p. 2.

5. Ferdinand de Saussure, *Cours de linguistique générale,* pp. 226–227.

6. Noam Chomsky, *Language and Mind,* p. viii.

7. From *The Philosophical Works of Descartes,* translated and edited by Elizabeth Haldane and G. R. Ross (Cambridge, Eng.: Cambridge University Press, 1932), pp. 116–17.

8. Etienne de Coudillac, *Essai sur l'origine, des connaissances humaines,* p. 6.

9. Section IV, chapter 1, in ibid., p. 75.

10. Section I, chapter 1, in ibid., p. 10.

11. Quoted in *The Mathematical Experience,* by P. J. Davis and Reuven Hersh(Boston: Birkhaüser, 1981), p. 113 (my italics).

12. René Descartes, *Œuvres,* I, p. 634.

13. V. N. Volochinov, *Marxism and Philosophy of Language,* p. 9.

14. Charles S. Peirce, *Selected Writings,* p. 180.

15. Ibid., p. 389.

16. Ibid., pp. 51–52.

17. Henri Bergson, *Œuvres,* p. 613; English translation by A. Mitchell: *Creative Evolution* (New York: The Modern Library), pp. 153–54.

18. Bergson, *Œuvres,* p. 614; *Creative Evolution,* p. 155. Hereafter in this section the page references from these two sources are given in the text.

19. Heidegger, *Being and Time,* p. 209.

20. Heidegger, *The Basic Problem of Phenomenology,* p. 164.

21. Ibid., p. 165.

22. Heidegger, *Being and Time,* p. 116.

23. See William R. Parzynski and Philip W. Zipse, *Introduction to Mathe-*

*matical Analysis* (New York: McGraw-Hill, 1981), Chap. 1, "Sets and Functions," pp. 1–5.

24. Quoted in Ian Hacking, *Representing and Intervening*, p. 123.

## *Meditation Five*

1. René Char, *Œuvres complètes* (Paris: Gallimard, Bibliothèque de la Pléiade, 1983), p. 411.

2. Char, *Œuvres,* p. 344.

3. I would like to mention Ora Avni's recent work, *The Resistance of Reference*. I hope I am not betraying the dominant aim of her exciting research if I say that her problematics and mine have a few elements in common: first, our awareness of the deadlock that characterizes philosophies of language in our century; second, the crucial significance of literature for a reexamination of the theories of language, particularly how referents such as female genitals, wedding ring, diamond studs, and such, put to a severe test Frege, de Saussure, Russell, Benveniste, and others, revealing the limits of their theoretical explanations. I can but applaud the following statement: "The literary text benefits from a freedom unknown to the theoretical text (p. 266)." Such is the new duty of the literary critic: to go beyond the deconstructive analysis and to find out the beauties and depths of artistic creation. However, I believe that to be able to apprehend the freedom of language, rewriting the theoretical language itself is indispensable. One cannot reject theory and continue to use its basic concepts to show their limits! It is true indeed that literature cannot be integrated into the rigid frame of any kind of theoretical language; but it does not mean that theory proper should stop its own developments. If one wishes to base reference criticism on safe principles, theory requires its own criticism. It has been the main purpose of my present meditations.

# *Bibliography*

Amory, Ruth, and Elisheva Rosen. *Les Discours du cliché*. Paris: Sedes, 1982.

Arnauld, Antoine, and Claude Lancelot. *Grammaire générale et raisonnée de Port-Royal*. Geneva: Slatkine Reprints, 1972.

Auerbach, Eric. *Mimesis: The Representation of Reality in Western Literature*. Translated by W. R. Trask. Princeton, N.J.: Princeton University Press, 1953.

Avni, Ora. *The Resistance of Reference: Linguistics, Philosophy and the Literary Text*. Baltimore, Md.: The Johns Hopkins University Press, 1990.

Bakhtin, Mikhael M. *The Dialogic Imagination: Four Essays*. Austin: University of Texas Press, 1981.

Baker, Gordon P., and Peter M. S. Hacker, *Language, Sense and Nonsense: A Critical Investigation into Modern Theories of Language*. Oxford: Basil Blackwell, 1984.

Banfield, Ann. *Unspeakable Sentences: Narration and Representation in the Language of Fiction*. London: Routledge and Kegan Paul, 1982.

Barthes, Roland. "Introduction à l'analyse structurale des récits." *Communications* 8 (November 1966).

———. "L'effet de réel." *Communications* 11 (1968).

Bataille, Georges. *L'Expérience intérieure*. Paris: Gallimard, 1943.

Baudelaire, Charles. *Œuvres complètes,* I. Paris: Gallimard, 1975.

Beckett, Samuel. *Compagnie*. Paris: Editions de Minuit, 1980.

———. *L'Innommable*. Paris: Editions de Minuit, 1953.

———. *Three Novels*. New York: Grove Press, 1965.

Benjamin, Walter. *Illuminations*. Edited by Hannah Arendt. Translated by Harry Zohn. New York: Schocken Books, 1968.

Benveniste, Emile. *Indo-European Language and Society*. Translated by Elizabeth Palmer. Miami: University of Miami Press, 1973.

———. *Problèmes de linguistique générale I*. Paris: Gallimard, 1966.

Bergson, Henri. *Creative Evolution*. New York: The Modern Library, 1944.

———. *Œuvres*. Paris: Presses Universitaires de France, 1963.

Berkeley, George. *Philosophical Writings*. New York: Collier Books, 1965.

Blanchard, Marc Eli. *Saint-Just & Cie: La Révolution et les mots*. Paris: Librairie A.-G. Nizet, 1980.

Bréal, Michel. *Essai de sémantique (Science des significations)*. 3d ed. Paris: Hachette, 1904.

Breton, André. *Le Surréalisme et la peinture*. Paris: Gallimard, 1966.

Brooks, Peter. *Reading for Plot: Design and Invention in Narrative*. New York: Knopf, 1984.

Cixous, Hélène. *La Venue à l'écriture* (with Annie Leclerc and Madeleine Gagnon). Paris: Union Générale d'Edition, 10/18, 1977.

Chisholm, Roderick. *An Essay on Reference and Intentionality*. Minneapolis: University of Minnesota Press, 1981.

Chomsky, Noam. *Aspects of the Theory of Syntax*. Cambridge, Mass.: MIT Press, 1965.

———. *Language and Mind*. New York: Harcourt, Brace & World, 1968.

———. *Rules and Representations*. New York: Columbia University Press, 1980.

———. *Communications, Language and Meaning: Psychological Perspectives*. Edited by A. Miller. New York: Basic Books, 1973.

Condillac, Etienne de. *Essai sur l'origine des connaissances humaines*. Paris: Armand Colin, 1924 (1st ed., 1746).

Culler, Jonathan. *Ferdinand de Saussure*. Ithaca, N.Y.: Cornell University Press, 1986.

Damish, Hubert. *Théorie du nuage: Pour une histoire de la peinture*. Paris: Editions du Seuil, 1972.

Davidson, Donald, and Gilbert Hartman, eds. *Semantics of Natural Languages*. Boston: Reidel Publishing Company, 1972.

De Man, Paul. *Allegories of Reading*. New Haven, Conn.: Yale University Press, 1979.

Descartes, René. *Œuvres*. Paris: Garnier, 1963.

Descombes, Vincent. *Objects of All Sorts: A Philosophical Grammar*. Translated by Lorna Scott-Fox and Jeremy Harding. Baltimore, Md.: The Johns Hopkins University Press, 1986.

Egger, Victor. *La Parole intérieure*. Paris: Alcan, 1904.

Evans, Gareth. *Collected Papers*. Oxford: Clarendon Press, 1986.

———. *The Varieties of Reference*. Edited by John McDowell. Oxford: Oxford University Press, 1982.

Felman, Shoshana. *The Literary Speech Act: Don Juan with Austin, or Seduction in Two Languages*. Ithaca, N.Y.: Cornell University Press, 1984.

Fish, Stanley. *Is There a Text in This Class? The Authority of Interpretative Communities*. Cambridge, Mass.: Harvard University Press, 1980.

Fodor, Jerry A. *The Modularity of Mind: An Essay on Faculty Psychology*. Cambridge, Mass.: MIT Press, 1983.

Frege, Gottlob. *Philosophical Writings*. Translated by Max Black. Oxford: Basil Blackwell, 1960.

Geach, Peter Thomas. *Mental Acts: Their Contents and Their Objects*. London: Routledge and Kegan Paul, 1957.

———. *Reference and Generality: An Examination of Some Medieval and Modern Theories*. Ithaca, N.Y.: Cornell University Press, 1980.

Gilson, Etienne. *Le Réalisme méthodique*. Paris: Chez Pierre Tequi, 1936.

———. *L'Etre et l'essence*. Paris: Vrin, 1948.

Girard, René. *La Violence et le sacré*. Paris: Grasset, 1972.

Goodman, Nelson. *Languages of Art: Approach to a Theory of Symbols*. New York: Merrill, 1968.

———. *Of Mind and Other Matters*. Cambridge, Mass.: Harvard University Press, 1984.

———. *Ways of Worldmaking*. Indianapolis: Hackett, 1978.

Greimas, Algirdas J., and Joseph Courtès. *Sémiotique: Dictionnaire raisonné de la théorie du langage*. Paris: Hachette, 1979.

Green, Julien. *Le Langage et son double*. Paris: Edition de la différence, 1985.

Hacking, Ian. *Representing and Intervening: Introductory Topics in the Philosophy of Natural Sciences*. Cambridge, Eng.: Cambridge University Press. 1983.

Hamelin, Octave. *Essai sur les éléments principaux de la représentation*. Paris: Alcan, 1907.

Hegel, Georg W. F. *Phenomenologie des Geistes*. Stuttgart: Friedrich Fromman Verlag, 1964.

Heidegger, Martin. *The Basic Problems of Phenomenology*. Bloomington: Indiana University Press, 1982.

———. *Being and Time*. Translated by J. Macquarrie and E. Robinson. New York: Harper & Row, 1962.

Hume, David. *A Treatise of Human Nature*. New York: Dutton, 1977 (1st ed., 1739).

Husserl, Edmund. *Cartesian Meditations*. The Hague: M. Nijhoff, 1960 (1st ed., 1932).

James, Henry. *Henry James*. Edited by R. P. Bakmur. New York: Scribner, 1934.

Jaume, Lucien. *Le Discours jacobin et la démocratie*. Paris: Fayard, 1989.

Kant, Emmanuel. *Œuvres philosophiques*. Paris: Gallimard, Bibliothèque de la Pléiade, 1980–86.

Kripke, Samuel A. *Naming and Necessity*. Cambridge, Mass.: Harvard University Press, 1980.

———. *Wittgenstein on Rules and Private Language*. Cambridge, Mass.: Harvard University Press, 1982.

Kritzman, Lawrence D. *The Rhetoric of Sexuality and the Literature of the French Renaissance*. Cambridge, Eng.: Cambridge University Press, 1991.

Lalande, André. *Vocabulaire technique et critique de la philosophie*. 7th ed. Paris: Presses Universitaires de France, 1956.

Le Senne, René. *Introduction à la philosophie*. 5th ed. Paris: Presses Universitaires de France, 1970.

Lewis, K. David. *Counterfactuals*. Cambridge, Mass.: Harvard University Press, 1973.

*Littérature et réalité*. Paris: Editions du Seuil, 1982.

Locke, John. *An Essay Concerning Human Understanding*. Oxford: Clarendon Press, 1975 (1st ed., 1690).

Lyons, John. *Introduction to Theoretical Linguistics*. Cambridge, Eng.: Cambridge University Press, 1968.

———. *Semantics*. Cambridge, Eng.: Cambridge University Press, 1977.

———. *Language and Linguistics*. Cambridge, Eng.: Cambridge University Press, 1981.

Lyotard, Jean-François. *Le Différend*. Paris: Editions de Minuit, 1983.

Mallarmé, Stéphane. *Œuvres*. Paris: Gallimard, Bibliothèque de la Pléiade, 1945.

Marr, David. *Vision: A Computational Investigation into the Human Representation and Processing of Visual Information*. New York: Freeman, 1982.

Martinet, André. *Eléments de linguistique générale*. Paris: Armand Colin, 1967.

Meillet, Antoine. *Introduction à l'étude comparée des langues indoeuropéennes*, 8th ed. Paris: Hachette, 1937.

Merleau-Ponty, Maurice. *Le Visible et l'invisible*. Paris: Gallimard, 1964.

———. *Prose du monde*. Paris: Gallimard, 1969.

Millikan, Ruth G. *Language, Thought and other Biological Categories: New Foundations for Realism*. Cambridge, Mass.: MIT Press, 1984.

Morot-Sir, Edouard. "Texte, Référence et Déictique," *Texte* 1 (1982).

Nicod, Jean. *Geometry and Induction*. Translated by John Bell and Michael Woods. Berkeley: University of California Press, 1970.

Parzynski, William R., and Philip W. Zipse, *Introduction to Mathematical Analysis*. New York: Hill, 1982.

Pascal, Blaise. *Œuvres complètes*. Paris: Editions du Seuil, 1963.

Peirce, Charles S. *Selected Writings (Values on a Universe of Chance)*. New York: Dover Publications, 1958.

Popper, Karl R., and John C. Eccles. *The Self and Its Brain. An Argument for Interactionism*. New York: Springer International, 1977.

Putnam, Hilary. *Mind, Language and Reality*. Cambridge, Eng.: Cambridge University Press, 1975.

———. *Reason, Truth and History*. Cambridge, Eng.: Cambridge University Press, 1981.

———. *Realism and Reason*. Cambridge, Eng.: Cambridge University Press, 1981.

Quine, Willard. *Word and Object*. Cambridge, Mass.: Harvard University Press, 1960.

Renou, Louis. *Hymnes spéculatifs du Véda*. Paris: Gallimard, 1956.

Ricoeur, Paul. *Temps et récit*. Paris: Editions du Seuil, 1983.

Riffaterre, Michael. *The Semiotics of Poetry*. Bloomington: Indiana University Press, 1978.

*The Rig Veda*. New York: Penguin Classics.

Roget, Peter Mark. *Thesaurus of Words and Phrases*. New ed., revised and enlarged by Samuel R. Roget. New York: Grosset & Dunlap, 1974.

Rorty, Richard. *Consequences of Pragmatism.* Minneapolis: University of Minnesota Press, 1982.

———. *Objectivity, Relativism, and Truth: Philosophical Papers.* Vol. 1. Cambridge, Eng.: Cambridge University Press, 1991.

Rousseau, Jean-Jacques. *Œuvres complètes.* Vol. I. Paris: Gallimard, Bibliothèque de la Pléiade, 1959.

Russell, Bertrand. *Logic and Knowledge: Essays 1901–1950.* Edited by R. C. Marsh. London: George Allen and Unwin, 1956.

Ryle, Gilbert. *The Concept of Mind.* London: Hutchinson and Company, 1949.

Salmon, Nathan. *Reference and Essence.* Princeton, N.J.: Princeton University Press, 1981.

Sartre, Jean-Paul. *L'Idiot de la famille.* Vol. II. Paris: Gallimard, 1971.

Saussure, Ferdinand de. *Cours de linguistique générale.* Paris: Payot, 1976. (1st ed., 1916).

———. *Course in General Linguisitics.* Translated by Wade Baskin. New York: McGraw-Hill, 1959.

Searle, John. *Intentionality: An Essay in the Philosophy of the Mind.* Cambridge, Eng.: Cambridge University Press, 1983.

———. *Mind, Brain and Science.* Cambridge, Mass.: Harvard University Press, 1984.

———. *Speech Acts: An Essay in the Philosophy of Language.* Cambridge, Eng.: Cambridge University Press, 1969.

Strawson, Peter F. *Individuals: An Essay in Descriptive Metaphysics.* Garden City, N.Y.: Anchor Books, 1963.

———. *Skepticism and Naturalism: Some Varieties.* New York: Columbia University Press, 1985.

Voloshinov, Viktor N. *Marxism and the Philosophy of Language.* Translated by Ladislas Matejka and I. R. Titunik. New York: Seminar Press, 1973 (1st ed. in Russian, 1930).

Vygotsky, L. S. *Thought and Language.* Edited and translated by E. Hamfam and G. Vakar. New York: Wiley, 1962.

Whorf, Benjamin L. *Language, Thought and Reality.* Cambridge, Eng.: Cambridge University Press, 1956.

Wittgenstein, Ludwig. *Tractatus Logico-Philosophicus.* London: Routledge and Kegan Paul, 1971 (1st ed., 1922).

———. *Philosophical Grammar.* Oxford: Oxford University Press, 1974.

———. *Philosophical Investigations.* New York: Macmillan, 1973. (1st edit., 1953).

# *Index*